The Handoff:
A Stoic Guide to Your Heroic Journey

by Alexander Clark

© Copyright 2024 Alexander Clark

ISBN 979-8-88824-262-9

All rights reserved. No part of this publication may be reproduced, stored in a retrieval system, or transmitted in any form or by any means—electronic, mechanical, photocopy, recording, or any other—except for brief quotations in printed reviews, without the prior written permission of the author.

Published by

3705 Shore Drive
Virginia Beach, VA 23455
800-435-4811
www.koehlerbooks.com

THE HANDOFF

A Stoic Guide to Your Heroic Journey

ALEXANDER CLARK

VIRGINIA BEACH
CAPE CHARLES

TABLE OF CONTENTS

INTRODUCTION...1

CHAPTER 1..5

CHAPTER 2..18

CHAPTER 3..34

CHAPTER 4..48

CHAPTER 5..57

CHAPTER 6..75

CHAPTER 7..88

CHAPTER 8..103

CHAPTER 9..115

CHAPTER 10..128

CONCLUSION..145

ACKNOWLEDGMENTS......................................150

INTRODUCTION

WHAT I THINK IS THAT A GOOD LIFE IS ONE HERO JOURNEY AFTER ANOTHER. OVER AND OVER AGAIN, YOU ARE CALLED TO THE REALM OF ADVENTURE.

—JOSEPH CAMPBELL

Whenever you pick up a book, whether you know it or not, you are entering into a contract. You, as the reader, are offering your time and money in exchange for knowledge. The author receives your money but gains something else in return: confirmation that their creative muse has inspired something of value for others.

The contract you and I will enter at the very beginning of this book, and that will remain with us until it is finished, is simple. The promise is this: I will meet you at the end. I don't know what it is you will learn because my suspicion is that it will be uniquely personal to you and only you. Whatever you will learn can literally change your life forever . . . if you let it. But no matter where you are by the end, I'll meet you there.

Along the way, I will use examples from my life to help highlight some principles that I think might serve you at some place in your future. I don't think I occupy any special position to be able to tell you how to live, how to think, or how to feel. My life is not an extraordinary example of enlightenment. It is with absolute humility that I offer some of my experiences to you, so that not only might you learn from them, but you might elevate yourself beyond my position when I encountered them. Use my life as a stepping stool to reach higher heights. Shorten the learning cycle. After all, wisdom is the ability to learn from *other* people's mistakes.

Throughout the book, I will introduce stoicism as a tool for you to use, if you would like, to help build yourself into a resilient and capable person. Ultimately, you will choose whether or not you wish to apply stoic principles to your life as you navigate its obstacles and challenges.

Stoicism is a philosophy that offers its practitioners a chance at peace on earth. Stoicism is a collection of Western ideas that spans the breadth of time—from the ancient era to our contemporary times—grounded in the pursuit of ending unnecessary suffering. There are thinkers who have shaped the philosophy, but they are not divinely backed prophets who have a monopoly on truth. Traditional Stoic philosophers were men who made mistakes in their personal lives and who were undoubtedly products of the ancient culture they lived in—relics in many ways, with certain customs and practices that are not only antiquated but repulsive to our modern standards. My recommendation is that we don't throw the baby out with the bath water. Truth has existed as long as mankind has, but our approach to it has varied by culture, by time period, and by the collective knowledge available to us.

Stoicism is not a cult nor a religion. You make no public profession of acceptance of it, nor are there symbols that link you to it other than the ones you craft in your own mind. There is no tithe or political agenda that supports it. It exists unseen as the most powerful expression a person can have; it exists as an idea. And ideas grow at the speed of light, acting as the life force within us all. An idea is the most powerful possession a person can ever have.

The chapters in this book are designed to take you on a journey of discovery. You will learn more about me and about stoicism, but the most important subject of the story is you. You have been front

INTRODUCTION

and center in my mind as I've spent years writing this book. You are found within these pages. You exist within the lines and words that are bound between the covers of this book. At the end of the book, when you turn the last page, we will end our journey together. But in many ways, we will have just started.

Wherever you are in life, I hope this book meets you with the perfect timing that only Fate herself knows how to deliver. I hope that no matter your age, sex, race, or nationality, this book can find you just as you are and help make you into all you can be. I originally wrote this book as a tool for young people who wanted to join the military. But as each draft of the manuscript took hold and the character of the book changed, I found that the audience had expanded to include adults, civilians, and the amateur philosopher. If the book is given as a graduation gift for someone who has just completed high school or college, I hope that the parents have read the book as well. If you are young, then this book will encourage you to chase after your dreams. If you are older, then this book will remind you to chase after your dreams even if you have done the sensible thing and abandoned them.

You will leave this book with a kick in the rear to get out into the world and be the hero you are meant to be. To become a well-adjusted person who can make a difference in the lives of those you love. And it is my hope that I can expand, just a little bit, the capacity you might think you have for love.

The final note to mention is my use of the word "hero." It is a loaded word. It conjures powerful images of inspiration of the pinnacle of bravery and excellence, unobtainable by the masses. We have all picked different heroes in our lives—men and women who have inspired us by their extraordinary example. We also have shared heroes. Soldiers, sailors, marines, and airmen who have died in defense of our freedom. Firefighters and policemen who respond to emergencies in our communities. Doctors and nurses who save lives day in and day out. Leaders in our community who have overcome socioeconomic challenges and emerged as role models for others to do the same.

Joseph Campbell was an American professor who wrote the book *The Hero with a Thousand Faces*. His thesis makes the argument that around the world and across cultures and time, mankind has developed a universal hero archetype. He believes there is a journey every hero—man or woman—must undergo. There are steps that happen sequentially and there are steps that are interchangeable, but the hero's experiences culminate in shared processes of growth, failure, and redemption. These steps lay out the journey—the way ahead into the dark unknown of the world that even we mere mortals can follow.

In short, you are a hero.

If you are repulsed by the idea of calling yourself one, then this book is written exactly for you. If you are confused because you don't feel heroic, don't worry. The language throughout the book will clearly differentiate between a hero who has acted heroically in the traditional sense of the word and the heroic journey we must take as human beings.

Let's take this journey together. At the end of the book, we will pause before we leave our time together to look back on how far we've come. I'll point down the mountain and say to you, "Wow, look how high we've climbed!" and then you'll continue even further up the mountain on your own. You will ascend into the clouds, and I hope there you will rest. I hope that on the mountaintop of your life, you will earn a view that shocks you. I hope you are startled by the beauty of life, of the potential within you that you never knew existed.

I hope you find what every hero searches for: peace. The deep peace of a life well-lived. The lasting peace of a life of introspection. The divinely inspired peace that calls you home into the halls of heroes and the hunting grounds of our ancestors of old. The peace that opens wide the gates of paradise as the saints who are waiting for you thank you for the gifts you have shared with others.

But that's—God willing—a long, long time from now.

Let's take the first step of your heroic journey together by turning the page that will bring you into the now-intertwined story of our lives.

I will see you at the end.

CHAPTER 1

THE HERO'S JOURNEY ALWAYS BEGINS WITH THE CALL.

—JOSEPH CAMPBELL

I sat on a black leather couch in the station room, watching TV and drinking the one Cherry Coke I allowed myself to drink per week. At seventeen years old, I was the youngest and newest member of my emergency medical service (EMS) crew, and because of that title, I didn't get to pick what was on TV. Not that it mattered to me. I didn't spend my Saturday nights at the volunteer fire department so that I could watch my favorite TV show. I came for the action.

While some of my high-school classmates chased girls, drank booze, and experimented with drugs on Saturday nights, I was chasing a different high. I was chasing adrenaline, the hero's drug. That night, I didn't have to wait long for my hit.

Without a warning, the firehouse radio squelched over the intercom. A siren toned the familiar alarm that commanded our world to *stop*. We all waited for the dispatcher to announce what the call would be.

The voice was expressionless and robotic.

"Station 35, be advised, code twenty-three."

Internally, my own alarm bell began ringing. Code 23 meant a drug overdose. I felt my heart rate spike as epinephrine was released from my adrenal glands and coursed through my veins. My whole body jolted into a state of hypervigilance. Somewhere out there, in my own community, a life was fading. Now it was my chance to rise to the occasion and save that life. This was the call I had craved all week in class—the chance to prove myself to my EMS team and to myself.

Nothing made me feel more alive. Nothing blocked out all the stress and made me forget all the pressure of my life more than the hero's drug could. By responding to a drug overdose for illegal substances, I was riding the best high I could imagine. That eye-widening, blood-rushing energy surge was blissfully euphoric. And to no surprise, adrenaline is the body's self-created cocaine. It wasn't like going on a roller coaster or the adrenaline rush before a big game. It wasn't like anything I could replicate—not until the next call came in to save someone's life. Not only was I tapping into my body's evolutionary fight-or-flight response, I was tapping into a different part of my psyche. I was tapping into the primal desire to feel power. I wanted to save a life. I wanted to rob the Reaper and cheat Death. I wanted to pull someone on the brink of death back into the world of the living. I wanted to feel like a hero.

From an early age, I picked my grandfather as a hero. He was a Vietnam veteran—an artillery officer who completed two combat tours. He was a badass, and I knew it. I had already wanted to be a soldier my whole life, so it was natural that I wanted to be like my grandfather. Before he joined the Army, he paid his way through college by working as a forest firefighter in the mountains of Montana.

When I was around twelve years old, he took me to a fire department that had turned an entire room into a train garden as part of a Christmas fundraiser. It was awesome. I was in a fire station—with my grandfather—surrounded by firefighters who looked so cool. That's

CHAPTER 1

when I noticed a flyer on their bulletin board recruiting firefighters.

"I want to join!" I told my grandfather. It was too perfect. I could join the volunteer fire department before I joined the Army, just like him. The first step in my call to adventure: I could learn to be as brave and as tough and as strong as he was.

"I think you're too young, bud," he said. "Maybe when you are in high school you can join the volunteer fire department."

"Then I'm going to join when I'm old enough," I said, not realizing the power of promising your hero something like that. If you ever get the chance to tell your hero that you want to be like them, you have to at least try. From then on, my path felt set.

A part of us, deep down in our minds, is constantly looking to identify a hero. We may not all see heroes on the same path, because a hero is someone who embodies the ideals of whatever we value. Bravery is a trait that is universally admired, so it's natural for most of us to pick heroes in our lives who are the epitome of what we believe is brave. We often follow the people we identify as heroes, as well. They are the role models we hope one day to become—and they come from all walks of life. They come as men, and they come as women. They come in all shades of the human spectrum, across all walks of the human experience.

Heroes are ordinary people who do acts of service for others. They are soldiers, marines, sailors, coast guardsmen, and airmen. They are firefighters and policemen. They are nurses and doctors. Coaches and teachers. Mentors and role models. Veterans and civilians. They are your parents, and they are your neighbors down the street. The thing that all heroes have in common isn't what they look like or what job they do; it is one simple action they all took: they answered their calling.

As you try to figure out your heroic calling in life, I encourage you to look inside yourself first. Look at what you value. Look at what shaped you. Look at the painful memories, remembering the bad times and what made them so terrible. We've all been touched by the suffering of this world. For some of us, it happened before we were ready. We were caught off guard by pain, unprepared and defenseless. And the scars we earned at a young age have followed us through life. Somewhere inside that pain, locked away in the deep recesses of your heart, is a need no one has filled for you.

Pain is an indicator that the world isn't as it should be. If that pain persists, it is because your world hasn't changed. Chances are, your life's purpose and heroic journey will be linked to that trauma in some way. From your lowest moments you will find strength inside yourself that you can share with others to help them on their own journey. And that process of struggle, strength, and sharing is how we can change the world.

You might not believe that you have it in you. After all, who knows you better than you? You know every single one of the mistakes you have ever made. You know your insecurities. You know the flaws you hide from the world, and you worry that if you were to try something brave, all those hidden places will be revealed. That you will fail, and everyone will see you for who you really are.

Or maybe all of this talk of trauma doesn't resonate at all. You feel like you've lived a sheltered life, so you struggle to understand what makes you worthy of that path—born into a free society where your every need was provided for by your parents. Your privilege is your guilt, and you are crushed by the weight of your perceived debt to humanity for the great stroke of luck you've had. The fact of the matter is that for every single person born on this earth to realize their potential, they have to integrate their life with their own hero's journey. And the first step to becoming a hero is to hear the call and then answer it—no matter where you are when the call comes.

Four years after my conversation with my grandfather, my desire to join the volunteer fire department resurfaced. I was finishing up my sophomore year in high school. I had just taken the Advanced Placement test for a world history course, and my class had the rest of the day off. A group of friends and I decided we would walk to a local pizza joint that had the best pizza in town. I often joked that there

CHAPTER 1

was so much grease on their pizza that they should put a drowning warning on the box. It was a great way to celebrate the end of a hard class. I wasn't looking for anything but a good time.

We walked on the sidewalk alongside a busy road. I felt the momentum of passing cars breeze past me at forty or fifty miles per hour like sudden gusts of wind. With no crosswalk or stoplight for us to cross to get to the restaurant, the first group of us crossed without a problem. But when the second group tried to cross, one of my friends didn't look both ways. She was in the second group behind me, and I watched her fly through the air in front of me like a crumpled rag doll. I couldn't understand how a human body could move in such a way—fly so high into the air and slide so far on the pavement. My mind couldn't register what I was seeing. But then I heard it. The bone-crushing, plastic-breaking thud of a human body colliding with a speeding vehicle. Hard braking and the screeching sound of tires concluded the symphony of horror that had crashed into our world. Literally.

Her body lay crumpled across the two solid yellow lines that separated traffic.

Without thinking, I ran into the road to block oncoming traffic, my feet crunching broken plastic from the car with each step. I turned back to see our group of friends still frozen on the sidewalk, wide-eyed and open-mouthed, their bodies locked in stiff disbelief as they stared at the motionless body of our friend.

"Jimmy!" I yelled from the middle of the road. "Call 911!"

He snapped out of it and reached into his pocket, tapped the screen of his phone, and the call went through.

I turned to my friend on the ground. She was bleeding, her clothes and skin shredded from the impact of the collision and the long, terrible slide on the pavement. My outstretched arm was keeping her from getting run over again, halting the oncoming lane, but I didn't know what else to do. I couldn't actually help her. I didn't know anything about medicine. I didn't know how to stop bleeding, check for a pulse, give CPR, or put on a tourniquet. I was just a teenager walking to eat pizza.

Just then, a cop showed up. He was several cars back and had seen the accident. I called out to him.

"My friend just got hit by a car!" I said, then pointed to Jimmy. "He's on the line with 911."

"Give them my badge number." The gold badge on his chest glinted in the daylight. "Tell them I'm on scene and to send EMS."

I walked with him toward my friend. Without saying anything, he took his jacket off and draped it over her body. He looked like a father tucking in his child after reading a bedtime story.

"She's breathing," he said. "We'll need to keep her warm. I don't see any arterial bleeding, but I don't want to move her."

Some of her girlfriends came over and sat beside her in the middle of the street. Their hands gently patted her bloody and matted hair, letting her know she wasn't alone. We waited for the ambulance to arrive. We heard sirens, and moments later, a white and red ambulance with big letters that read *Volunteer Fire Department* arrived on scene, "packaged" her up, and took her to the hospital.

The ambulance reminded me of my promise to my hero. I was sixteen and old enough to join. And now I had seen them in action.

I wanted to help people the way they helped my friend.

It took a while for my friend to recover. She broke her pelvis and had several other extensive injuries. But she lived and she walked again. Although it was a tragic event, I realized it was just one of countless emergencies that had happened in my community on that single day. Every day, terrible things happen. Every day, people reach moments of crisis and dial 911 for the help they are incapable of giving themselves. I didn't want to be helpless the next time an emergency showed up in my life. I didn't want to have to call 911. I wanted to become a man who was capable of handling his own problems and those of others.

When we are young, the world is full of potential. We can be anything we want to be. I had played sports, I had joined clubs, I had worked odd jobs here and there. Until the accident, I had gotten distracted from my heroic journey. It's not that your heroic journey

CHAPTER 1

can't take you on the path of excelling in academics and sports, but I knew that wasn't my purpose. I knew that I had been called to help people. There had been a stirring in my heart when I saw those firefighters four years earlier. The idea of becoming one had sparked something inside my soul that remained dormant until it demanded to be heard. It was an inescapable force. I could run, I could hide, but I could never be free from the pull of it in my bones.

The heroic journey unveils itself to a willing soul. It is love at first sight and the instant deep connection to a version of yourself that doesn't exist yet. For some people, the call is a soft whisper, heard each night in their dreams when their minds surrender to the potential of who they might become. For others it is a door slammed in their face. For others it is a trumpet blaring in their ears almost every moment of every day. I saw my calling as vividly as if I were living it in real life. It was a vision of sorts—a premonition.

That night after my friend's accident I printed off the volunteer fire department's application online. Within a month I was accepted into the department and was doing ride-alongs. I wanted to make a difference. I was chock full of idealism, purpose, and drive to make a positive impact in my community. I didn't know what the price would be in my own life.

The last two years of high school became some of the most formative years of my life. I was a first responder to heart attacks, strokes, suicides, domestic violence, gang violence, drug overdoses, car crashes, and a myriad of other emergencies in my community. Those calls came at a price, an invisible scarring that took a long time to recover from. My heart was in the right place, but I wasn't mature enough. I wasn't ready to handle what was thrown at me. I knew I was giving up my Saturday nights as a teenager—that's a price tag that's easy enough to understand. I wasn't going to have the fun most high-school kids had at my age. I figured that I was going to go through a rite of passage and that I was willingly initiating my transformation from a boy to a man.

But the cost of being a man isn't always known to the boy.

I didn't read Bessel van der Kolk's book *The Body Keeps the Score* until it was too late. I didn't know that I could be in horrific situations and that those horrors were going to be literally absorbed into my nervous system. I didn't know that the calls would follow me for years and cause me infinitely more pain later than I experienced in the brief moments the calls had lasted. The real price of my EMT work wasn't giving up my carefree teenage years; it was that I would waste a decade avoiding real intimacy, willfully engaging in self-destructive behavior, and developing an inner critic that would talk to me in ways I would never speak to another person, nor let someone else speak to me.

This is what happens to people whose work—whose calling—exposes them to trauma. But I didn't have a worldview in place that could serve as a buttress against it. I thought my sense of compassion was enough. Some of us see suffering and want to do something about it. But the world is a messy place, and compassion isn't always enough—especially when you're young and have so much to learn. My sense of compassion became a double-edged sword. It made me vulnerable to the other side of EMT work.

When someone calls 911, it is because they are having the worst day of their life. Something is happening to them that they are unable to respond to. They need help. I was their help. I had to have the answers to their crisis. But I didn't know how to make sense of their suffering either—and I didn't know how to recover after particular grueling calls. Like an infectious disease, the pain of EMT calls infected me secondhand. I just showed up, did my job, and went home every Saturday night for two years, until my worldview developed into something that could help me make sense of a complex, unfair world. *If not me, then who?* became a self-flagellating mantra that kept me in the game, playing through injuries I didn't even realize I had.

CHAPTER 1

When that alarm sounded in the firehouse, it jolted me out the world in which I was just a kid in high school. I sprang into action as an EMT, not as a seventeen-year-old-kid—and not waiting to hear the address. That was Lou's job. He was the driver, and the best one in the department. I knew he would figure out the route from the station to the location of the overdose. I ran into the engine bay, grabbed my black Under Armour gloves and hat, and hopped into the back of the red and white ambulance. A moment later, the bay doors opened, and the ambulance pulled out onto the road and began its solemn wail as Lou brought it to life.

I pulled my cap down over my ears, Under Armour logo centered on my forehead, and could hear my heart pumping in my head. I closed my eyes and leaned my head back against my seat as we sped toward the location of the call. I rehearsed in my mind what I was about to do.

I love this feeling, I thought to myself as we took a sharp turn and the ambulance stopped.

Lou turned off the siren. That was my cue to open up the ambo doors and jump out of the back carrying the blue and green medical bags, each weighing close to fifteen pounds and stuffed to bursting with medical supplies needed for the call.

I jumped out of the back and took in my surroundings. The ambulance was parked in a long driveway in a suburban neighborhood. I didn't know where I was. The call was outside of my home station's jurisdiction.

A woman was standing on her back porch, screaming, "He's inside! Hurry! Please God, save him!"

I tried to run with the heavy bags, one in each hand, but it turned into a shuffle as I walked up the stairs behind my crew and into her home.

Jon, the paramedic and third member of my crew, was an old pro. He had the most medical training and would take the lead on this call. He asked a stream of questions, trying to understand what we were getting into.

"Tell me what happened to your son," Jon said.

"I think he's overdosing, but I don't know what he took," the mother got out between sobs. Her daughter appeared and wrapped her arms around her mom. Our eyes met. I saw nothing inside of them. Certainly not hope.

She knows, I thought. Her brother was dying and there wasn't anything we could do to bring him back.

We rounded a corner and there he was, lying next to their dining room table. He was wearing jeans and a T-shirt, and his eyes were shut, his body totally relaxed as if he were sleeping.

I placed my blue bag on Jon's left, then walked to his right and placed the green bag down on the hardwood floor, making sure I didn't step over the patient. Operating on instinct, I knelt down, opened the blue bag, and placed an oximeter on his outstretched finger, his hands unresponsive to my touch. The oxygenation in his blood was alarmingly low. I checked for a pulse at his neck and found it weak and unreadable.

Jon keyed into the microphone of his radio.

"Dispatch, this is Unit 35. Be advised: call needs to be upgraded. Send Supervisor Six to call location. Over."

We had been in the home for less than a minute and already Jon had recognized that the patient needed more medical support than we could give him. Time was ticking. Jon handed the clipboard to me and got to work.

Now holding the clipboard, my job was to ask the mother and sister as many questions as I could and relay any pertinent information to Jon. It's usually best to keep family away from the paramedic, so I took a few steps backward out of the dining room and into their living room. The sister came into the room with me, but the mother didn't want to. She wanted to be next to her boy.

"Please ma'am, I have to ask you a few questions about your son," I said as gently as I could.

She looked down at her boy as Jon pulled up his shirt and attached

CHAPTER 1

electrodes to five parts of his torso. Her eyes came back to mine. She walked forward and collapsed into a chair in their living room, leaving her dying son behind her.

"Ma'am, what do you think he took?" I asked.

"I don't know. He's a soldier—he's not supposed to do drugs." Her voice gave out as grief brought forth something more animal than human. She would need a moment. I shifted my questions to the sister. She was my age or close to it. Thank God I didn't recognize her from my high school.

"Do you know if it could have been heroin or pain pills?"

"I don't know. He's on leave and just got back from a deployment. He turned twenty last week. He's been hanging out with his old high-school friends—I know one of them uses heroin," she said.

That was enough for me. I walked over to Jon and said, "It might be opioids."

"Right. Getting Narcan ready," Jon said.

It's standard procedure to give a patient Narcan if opioids are suspected as the cause of the overdose. Also called naloxone, Narcan blocks the brain's uptake of opioids. This allows the brain to send signals to the body to tell it to breathe again. Most brains will suffer permanent damage at four minutes without oxygen. Death can occur in as little as four to six minutes. It takes two to three minutes to know whether it works. John placed the young soldier's head into a neutral position and tipped it back. He placed the Narcan canister into one of the soldier's nostrils and pushed the plunger down, expelling the contents into his nose.

Just then, the supervisor came in with another ambulance crew. Technically, we had responded to a call outside of our jurisdiction, so the new crew would transport the soldier to the hospital. We had another call coming in for our own part of town. It was time for us to leave.

I handed off the information for the report and walked outside as Jon and Lou debriefed the incoming guys. I stood under the night sky and felt the cold creep onto my back. I wondered what demons had chased down the soldier to where he felt his only option was to numb himself to life. Did he see combat on his first deployment? Was he one of the twenty-two veterans a day who are reported to commit suicide? My breath hung in a misty cloud like an exhaled cigarette. He was only three years older than me. *This can't be my future*, I thought. *This can't be what happens to me.*

I had sweated through my undershirt, and as the adrenaline wore off I felt my hands start to shake. I put them in my pockets and waited for my crew to join me at the ambulance. It was just another night in January.

My life plan was to go to college, commission in the Army as a second lieutenant in the infantry and join a military fighting its fifteenth year in the Global War on Terror. *This is what you signed up for*, I scolded myself as I hopped into the back of the ambulance. *Seeing this stuff is what it takes to be a hero.*

"Do you think he'll make it?" I asked from the back of the ambulance.

The response was unanimous. "Nah. He's a goner."

I shivered again. This time it wasn't from the cold. It was because this call had just embedded itself into my soul. Suddenly, I was tired. I was seventeen. What was I doing running around town responding to nightmares? I knew my life wasn't normal, but this was way outside the scope of what most of my high-school classmates could comprehend. I felt lonely.

Whatever your calling is, only you can hear it—but you should know you aren't alone. I can't tell you the hero you will become. I can't tell you the journey you will take or the struggles that you will have to contend with along the way. Part of your heroic journey is the voyage into the unknown, however dangerous that may be. You will fight battles, and some of these battles you will have to fight on your own—on a path that feels like you alone are forging.

For some of us, that journey starts young. You've likely heard the first whispers of your calling. Are you listening? Maybe you've watched sports and wanted to become a professional athlete. You've watched

CHAPTER 1

movies and admired the strength of the actors that play the role of warriors. You've met teachers who inspired your passion for learning. You've seen celebrities on social media that portray the life you want to have. You've heard of people who've had a tremendous impact on the world and have wondered if you have anything of value to offer those around you. You have wondered if you have the strength to survive your journey, if you have what it takes.

CHAPTER 2

WE MUST LET GO OF THE LIFE WE HAD PLANNED, SO AS TO ACCEPT THE ONE THAT IS WAITING FOR US.

—JOSEPH CAMPBELL

The night my life truly changed began the same as every other night. The air conditioner hummed overhead as I sat on the couch in the firehouse, oblivious to the reality that the person I was would cease to exist just a few hours later.

With almost one year of EMT work under my belt I was still very much a rookie. But I knew this was the type of work that gave someone a purpose in life. I was hooked on the little drops of adrenaline that happened on calls. When I wasn't at the firehouse, I was thinking about the potential calls I might get the next time I took a shift. All through the week, I didn't think about my high-school sports or anything my friends were doing. I stopped focusing in school. I did enough work to earn decent grades, but I didn't apply myself. My "Saturday night lights" were the ambulance tearing down the street, racing to help someone in need. I usually didn't have to wait long. But on that Saturday night, I began to fear the worst. The hours ticked by. The TV flashed its own lights and sounds in front of me, but it couldn't hold my attention. My

CHAPTER 2

knee bounced in frustration. It looked like there wasn't going to be a call that night. My hand turned into a fist in protest.

As soon as it happened, my legs stopped bouncing, my hands relaxed, and my mind flipped into instant focus. I sat on the edge of my seat.

Relief flooded over me as I leaned in to hear the call.

This could be the big one.

"Station 35, be advised: five-alarm fire in progress." It was instantly all hands on deck. It had to be—a five-alarm fire is the largest category of any fire-related emergency. It requires an enormous amount of manpower to fight. And to top it off, the fire was raging at a local ten-story hotel.

All the firefighters in the station geared up in seconds, and two engines left the bay at lightning speed. Inside the hotel, firefighters climbed floor after floor of stairs in a desperate attempt to make sure all of the guests had been evacuated. They sucked in air through their respirators as they worked, jacking their heart rates through the roof. They overheated underneath the layers of the fire-retardant gear they wore to protect themselves from the flames that licked at them from the burning walls and ceilings around them. They fought the flames with the heavy hoses they hauled up from the fire hydrants outside. They were engaged in a heroic struggle to save lives.

But all of the relief I had felt moments before dissipated into the silence of the empty engine bay. Since I wasn't a firefighter, this wasn't my call.

Even Lou and Jon, who were firefighters as well as EMTs, were gone. It was just me, Lou's wife Diana (the firehouse mom), their daughter, and a lieutenant who had shown up too late to get on the engine. I felt his disappointment. My leg started to bounce again as I settled into the couch and my eyes glazed over as I stared at the TV and settled back into waiting mode.

It was just me and the lieutenant, but we formed a two-person medical crew. He would be the driver and I would be the medical provider. I felt strange and out of place without my crew and with a boss that I didn't know. After a year of forming our own crew, I had learned to rely on Lou and Jon for more than just medical knowledge. They were rock-solid men.

Lou was only middle-aged but had been an EMT for as long as I had been alive. He had tan weathered skin and a thick mustache hiding his coffee- and tobacco-stained teeth. Some of the longer hairs that cascaded from his upper lip would blow around from the force of his breath when he spoke, like a wheat field blowing in a summer breeze. But that was a rare sight. He seemed to weigh and measure his words before he spoke them out into the world and as a result, never had much to say. He was calculated and cool under pressure. In two years, I can't remember a single time Lou lost his composure on a call. And we did a few things together that should have gotten under his skin. But that was Lou. He could have been a cowboy in another lifetime, with the grit to match.

Jon could have gone to Hollywood. His hair had grayed while he was a young man. The weird contrast between the full head of gray hair that he possessed and the wrinkles that had yet to form around his eyes could have made him Richard Gere's stunt double. He wore slim silver glasses that were fixed permanently in place in front of his steel-colored eyes, never sliding down his nose as glasses tend to do. Jon always showed up to work early and did his inventories of the ambulance diligently, always with the checklist, never taking for granted that he had done the same inspection every week for twenty or so years.

These were the men I called my teammates. I felt confident knowing they had my back. Like a well-oiled machine, we didn't use words to communicate. We simply knew what needed to happen on each call. But that night, my team was gone, and with it my sense of familiarity. The conditions were set for the perfect storm. And when a call came in for a heart attack, patient unresponsive, the winds started to blow.

This is it! I instinctively thought.

"Grab your bag!" the lieutenant yelled through a tightened throat, as I felt a surge of my good friend adrenaline. I wasn't going to be left out of the action after all.

I ran to the empty engine bay, tossed the blue med bag into the

CHAPTER 2

back of a pickup truck, and jumped into the shotgun seat. Then we were off, lights and sirens parting traffic on the road like Moses splitting the Red Sea.

"You're CPR-certified right?" the lieutenant asked over the sound of the siren.

"I'm certified," I said.

"Good. You're going to be the thumper," he ordered.

"I got it."

The "thumper" is the nickname given to the first responder tasked with giving chest compressions. The job was easy. No intubations, no medications, no distractions. Just compressions.

We drove the rest of the way in silence while a thousand thoughts raced through my mind. We listened to the updates from the scene as the lieutenant turned and burned our way to the call, wrapped up in his own silent conversation with himself.

When we arrived, the front door was open. The lieutenant shouted "EMS!" as we crossed the threshold. But he didn't have to.

The patient was on the floor in the living room. He lay on his back in between the couch and the TV in just his underwear and white sleeveless undershirt. His legs were spread wider than would be a comfortable sleeping position and his arms were splayed out like a scarecrow.

A woman stood nearby, crying. Her hands rotated from covering her face to grabbing fistfuls of her hair as she watched a police officer who had knelt at his side. With fingers interlaced, palm centered on his chest at the nipple line, he was giving the compressions I would soon take over.

The lieutenant looked at me and pointed to the body. I knelt down beside the patient to relieve the police officer. Right away, I noticed that the man looked peaceful, totally unaware of the strangers in his room, the sirens wailing outside, the screams of the woman next to him, and the sounds of the TV station still playing in the background. He had crossed the divide into another place—one that wasn't among the living.

I laced my fingers together, placed my palm on his chest, and felt his hair underneath my hands. I leaned over the patient so that my arms were straight, with my shoulders over my hands. *Remember the rhythm. You got this*, I coached myself. I knew once I started the compressions that by law I had to continue them until relieved by someone of equal or greater medical training. I was going to be the thumper. I was going to be the best thumper there ever was. I was going to save this man.

I started my compressions. His chest was springy and bounced back into its natural position after each compression. His belly wiggled with each rebound as I thumped at a rate of 120 beats per minute. I counted out loud so that another first responder kneeling by his head would hear my thirtieth repetition and artificially breathe with the bag valve mask two times before I continued thumping another thirty compressions.

I was completely focused. Tunnel-visioned. Time was nothing. All that mattered was that the face I was staring down at would soon wake up. The eyelids would flutter. His mouth would open and suck in air.

But it wasn't happening. They put two patches on his chest that were connected to an AED machine and shocked the patient. They injected him with adrenaline. I thumped away, artificially circulating his blood in an attempt to save him. To restore him to the life he had among us.

We rolled him onto a backboard and then lifted him onto the stretcher.

"Take a break until we get him in the back of the ambulance. You'll take over again on the ride to the hospital," my lieutenant said. "I'll meet you at the ER and take you back to the station." He would drive the pickup truck we had driven to the call while I gave compressions in the back of the ambulance.

I didn't understand why I had been kicked off the thumper role momentarily until I saw a much lighter woman hop on top of the stretcher and begin giving compressions, straddling the patient while a group of first responders wheeled them out of the house and into the ambulance.

I looked around the now-empty living room and began gathering

CHAPTER 2

up the supplies and trash that were left behind. I walked outside to the truck. The lights flashed eerily in the night, creating weird shadows and making faces light up in alternating red and blue hues.

It seemed like the whole neighborhood was outside watching the tragedy unfold. Like rubberneckers on a highway, except these people knew it was their neighbor who was getting medical attention. I walked to the back of the ambulance, but a woman stopped me before I got there.

"Is my dad going to make it?" she asked me. Her nose was running, her eyes red.

I wanted to tell her what she wanted to hear. I knew she wanted me to tell her that her father was going to pull through. That he would live. That the last conversation they'd had wouldn't be the last one they would ever have in her lifetime. But as confident as I'd been while counting thumps moments before, I fumbled for words.

"We are doing everything we can," I said lamely. I felt like a politician at a press conference. Another woman embraced the daughter as she turned away from me, crying even harder. I hopped in the back of the ambulance.

Game on.

I was already drenched in sweat when I took over the thumper role again and the ambulance sped away. My face dripped sweat onto his as I gave compressions. Fifteen more minutes to go.

The man had been intubated by then, so a tube came out of his mouth. There was an IV in his arm. It had taken a few sticks to get the vein, and drops of blood had splattered onto the ambulance floor. With each turn the ambulance took, we rolled in the back with the momentum of the turn like sailors tossed in a storm at sea. I did my best to keep my balance and give compressions on cadence.

At some point on the drive, I realized his chest wasn't springing back up with the same force that it had before. It felt tired and deflated. It felt like I was pushing down on dough, not his sternum. My eyes never left his face though. I could see the black and gray hair of his goatee. I saw the faded tattoos on his arms and shoulders. His body flailed limply with each turn, dead weight that rolled and shifted on the stretcher, making it hard for me to keep my hands centered on his chest.

Please, God, I prayed. *Save this man.*

It had been a while since I had last prayed, but I knew there was nothing more I could do for him. It would take a miracle to bring him back.

Nurses met us at the automatic sliding glass doors of the ER. I walked beside the stretcher, still giving compressions until the nurses took over. They wheeled him into their cardiac room. He was hooked up and shocked again. A doctor took charge and began directing the staff in one last final effort.

After a while, I heard the doctor say, "I'm calling it. Time of death—9:13 p.m." It had been less than two hours from when the call had come in to when the call was over with the final words marking the end of our efforts to save his life.

I waited in the break room while the lieutenant filled out the report. He made a joke that when it was his time to die, he didn't want to die with his boots on—he wanted to die in his underwear too. The break room felt small, so I walked into the hallway toward the exit. I wanted fresh air. I wanted to be alone.

"How are you doing, hon?" Sarah asked. She was an ER nurse I knew from the past year of EMT work. She was a few years older than me, blond-haired and still energetic at the front end of her shift.

"I'm doing all right. Long night. How are you?" I replied.

"Oh, I'm doing just fine. Want to smoke a cigarette?"

"No, thank you," I said walking through the sliding glass doors.

"Suit yourself," she said as she ducked into a patient's room and back to work.

The irony of nurses smoking baffled me as a teenager. How could someone who knows the health problems caused by habitual smoking choose to smoke—and do it at a hospital of all places? It makes sense now that I'm older. A cigarette can be an answer to an unanswered prayer.

CHAPTER 2

Back at the firehouse, the adrenaline dump hit me like a hangover. But this time, shame and guilt followed like a freight train. My inner critic had been born, and it started telling me that I was a failure. Over and over again, I replayed the moment when I had to tell the daughter I couldn't save her dad. I had failed her, and I had failed him. I sat back down on the black leather couch in the station room and stared at the TV. My rational brain told me that the odds of saving him were slim if not nil, but my heart and body (and critic) rejected that logic. My humanity reeled at the sight of a fellow human dying in front of his daughter. Every intention I'd had and every effort I'd given that night had been oriented toward achieving one outcome: to bring him back to life. The critic tortured me, reviewing every moment to see where I had made a mistake.

Sometimes we are the last people we should listen to.

Remember Diana, Lou's wife? She was the firehouse mom, which meant she was not an EMT or firefighter, but she chose to support her husband on Saturday nights by eating family dinner with their daughter at the station so that Lou wouldn't miss out on family time. While she and her daughter waited for Lou to come back from the fire at the hotel, instead of being concerned about her husband and the father of her child battling flames at the risk of his own life, she thought of me. I was the youngest member of the department, and she knew that the call wasn't sitting well with me.

"Are you all right?" she asked.

I lied. "I'm fine. Thanks."

Her mother's intuition knew I was lying, but she didn't push me. We sat in silence. I had no words to describe what was going on, and why would I share what I was feeling anyway? That wasn't what a man would do in this situation.

We all learn how to deal with stress from infancy, when we feel the stress of our mothers and absorb their anxieties as our own. Modeling our behavior after others is one of our most primal survival instincts. If our mentors and parents deal with stress a certain way, then that's how we learn our own decompression methods. Short of smoking with a nurse, there was no one for me to follow that night. Lou wasn't there to coach me through it. Jon wasn't there to show me his death ritual. I was alone, and the silence from those around me was filled with accusing shouts inside my own head.

The inner critic is a nasty creature. When there is no language to describe your pain, your fear, and your shame, trauma is encoded into you, and it becomes the precise location of your vulnerability. In the absence of language to form an explanation, the critic accuses, abuses, and extends the trauma long after the event is over. The critic captures us and keeps us trapped in his world, where we replay events over and over again until, like a hostage held captive, we learn to adopt his point of view as our own. A self-manufactured Stockholm Syndrome.

Words label everything we see, feel, and experience, yet after periods of trauma they are the hardest thing to summon. Without language, we don't have one of the pathways available to us to process events and find closure. If we never learn how to process or articulate our experiences, we remain trapped in a wordless world where our emotions serve as the only relatable connection to the event. On the other hand, when we find the right words, we also find a path toward healing. A huge problem here is that men are notoriously silent creatures when it comes to pain. If I could rewrite that night in an alternate world, I would visit myself outside of that ER room. I'd tell my high-school self that a man doesn't need a fake wall around his heart to appear tough to others. That it's okay to feel, to be fully human and to experience the anguish of an unexpected death and the tragedy of it all. I'd tell him that the myth that a hero is a silent figure, stoic in the face of suffering to the point of total silence is bullshit. I'd tell him a stoic man isn't a silent one. Sure, a hero doesn't complain and whine and seek an audience to hear their pain, but neither does a hero suffer in silence.

Instead, I sat there, lying to someone who had tried to reach out to me, stewing in my own critic's shame. I wanted to wait for my crew to come back from the fire, but I couldn't. I had to get out of there before

CHAPTER 2

I lost it. I didn't want anyone to see me show weakness, so I left my shift before midnight and sped home, taking roads through deserted neighborhoods way too fast. I stepped out of my car, then stopped halfway up the driveway and threw up on the grass. All I could think about was how his chest felt at the end. It was like kneading raw meat before making a hamburger patty.

I snuck into the house without waking anyone up. I took a shower to get the smell of him and his house off me. I lay in bed unable to sleep. My mind kept replaying the night's events.

I wasn't a hero.

Senior year was a rough one. The calls kept adding up. I responded to a car crash on the beltway. I responded to a mother who took a handful of pills and tried to kill herself in front of her two adolescent children. I responded to an orphanage where a teenage girl was restrained after she had violently attacked her caregivers and attempted to kill herself. I responded to a mental health hospital where a naked patient lay on a mattress in the middle of the corridor, catatonic and reeking of feces. I responded to a man who'd had a stroke in the middle of the night as he went to the bathroom and had to lie in a puddle of his own piss until help arrived almost twenty-four hours later. I responded to a wedding where a nun was unresponsive and barely breathing—the wedding guests gasped as I unceremoniously manhandled her onto the stretcher. Sometimes, trying to save a life isn't very polite.

I responded to a high-school teammate who had tried to drift his car in a neighborhood and had rolled it. He escaped by crawling out through the passenger side window. I didn't say a word to him, and all I could think was that I would have beaten the shit out of him if he had hit a kid playing in the street.

I responded to a deranged naked woman who had fallen down the stairs. Her caregiver sat in the cluttered hoarder's living room and smoked a cigarette while the woman bled from her head.

I responded to a grandmother who had dislocated her hip falling down the stairs. Her husband was more distraught than she was, and she tried to calm him by saying through her Eastern European accent that this wasn't as bad as childbirth.

After each call, my recovery routine was the same: a ruthless self-examination that would rival any communist tribunal. I examined what I did wrong, shamed myself for those blunders until I believed it was sufficient enough to not repeat them, then added the call to either the win or loss column. Soon, I lost the tally altogether. The negative won out. I was attached to a metric of success that was never going to be achievable. The critic always had his voice heard. At the same time, my life existed outside my EMT work as that of a normal high-school kid. I had as normal of an all-American high-school experience as they come. I played five sports in a high school of three thousand students and earned enough college credits through Advanced Placement courses to graduate as an academic sophomore in college.

A few weeks after the CPR call, a gut-wrenching rejection came on my very first step toward my decade-long plan to join the Army. I had planned to apply to the United States Military Academy at West Point and for a Reserve Officer Training Corps (ROTC) scholarship. But to gain that scholarship or get accepted to a federal service academy, you must first pass a medical board. As fate would have it, the Department of Defense Medical Exam Review Board (DoDMERB)—in their omniscient and bureaucratic socialistic review process—deemed my body inadequate for the military. I'm still a little salty about it. The letter was waiting for me in the mailbox one day after cross-country practice. There it was, bolded and in uppercase for absolute clarity.

UNQUALIFED.

It was the fall of my senior year, and my world was unraveling. The weight of losing patients as an EMT made me feel like a failure, my love life was in ruins (I had gotten dumped), and now this. I lay down on my bed and felt my world spin. My future was collapsing, and it was all because of me. I was allergic to beestings and DoDMERB had found out. I now had failure written into my DNA.

A young mind can become unhinged when a haunting past collides

CHAPTER 2

with a painful present and is crushed by a sense of hopelessness for the future. And who could blame these young people who find themselves stuck—few people are talking about the challenges young people encounter, and few young people have the words to talk about those challenges when given the opportunity. Rarely do we know the struggles heroes go through. We don't know what forged them and we only have a public highlight reel of easy successes to go off. Failure is unsettling when we encounter it.

I had always known that I had been allergic to bees. I don't remember my first reaction because I was too young, and I had been stung later in childhood without having a reaction at all. But the lingering thought—had I really outgrown my allergy?—kept me cautious. Every time a bee landed near me, the hair on the back of my neck would stand up. It's strange to think that little insect could be an instrument of death.

I didn't know how close I would come to dying from one of those flying stinging insects until the summer before I entered high school. I was chopping wood at my family's cabin in Maine. The cabin is on a beautiful, secluded, pristine lake where the water is so still in the morning it looks like glass. As I was splitting logs into firewood with an ax, something bumped into my face and stung me on my head.

"I just got stung!" I said, more frustrated that I wasn't going to be able to use a chainsaw for the first time than that I was in pain.

"Go inside and take a break," my dad said. As a retired infantry lieutenant colonel, that was his version of a sympathetic response. In the military, in similar situations we jokingly say, "Take a knee, drink water, and pull security." The cure for any minor ailment.

Inside the cabin, I sat down and took a sip of iced tea. I didn't think anything was wrong until my whole body began to itch. *Everything* itched. It felt like my skin turned into one giant mosquito bite. I got into the weirdest positions imaginable just to find some edge or corner of the table that could find the sweet spot. I looked like a black bear pole dancing on a pine tree. My brother came inside the cabin. Instead of making fun of me for letting a beesting stop me from chores, he ran outside and grabbed my dad. They both came in, took one look at me, and called the dogs, who were roaming in the woods. We had to get to the closest hospital, over twenty miles away on backcountry dirt roads, and fast.

Don't get me wrong. I was experiencing discomfort from the sting. But up to that point, I didn't feel like I was in any particular danger. That changed when I felt my throat start to close. It itched on the inside and when I felt air pass over it started to feel like I was breathing through a straw. Pressure formed in my head. I thought my eyes were open, but soon I couldn't see because my eyelids had swollen shut. My brother described my face as if my head had gained two hundred pounds. Together, we walked to the car and loaded our two dogs into the blue 2005 Dodge Durango. My father sped the whole way, deftly navigating through gates that blocked private property lines as fast as possible. Dust and rocks flew from under the tires as we raced against the clock.

With my vision blurred, my body rocked side to side by the turning truck. An additional symptom of anaphylactic shock is vomiting, and I had just eaten a box of IGA twisted noodle macaroni and cheese. I painted the inside of the car orange. Macaroni artifacts were behind the driver's visor, in the passenger-side glove compartment, and in the vents of the air conditioner. Ten years later, my brother was handed down the Durango and said he would still find caked bits of noodles in random places. Sometimes when he drove over a speed bump, a hidden noodle would dislodge itself and fall like an icicle.

In town, the one road leading to the hospital was under construction. Bumper-to-bumper traffic blocked our way. My dad laid on the horn and beeped his way through oncoming cars to swerve his way into the emergency room parking lot. My brother sat in the front seat staring at me, making sure that, as best as he could tell, I was alive.

Still unable to see and laboring to breathe, I leaned on my dad and brother as they carried me into the ER. The nurses worked fast and got an IV into my arm. Then a doctor started giving me medication

CHAPTER 2

through the IV, which brought instant relief. I felt my throat open and air naturally fill my lungs with each inhale. What was the medicine they gave me to fight anaphylactic shock? Sweet, sweet adrenaline.

Hours later, I was released from the hospital and my family treated me like royalty. Ordinarily, as the baby of the family, I wasn't given the adequate attention that I knew I deserved. But for the rest of the week I got to eat whatever I wanted whenever I wanted. I got to stay up late, watch war movies, and not make my bed. I soon forgot about the pain and panic of being stung by the bee. But just a few years later, the pain of that day still couldn't compare to the pain of rejection that it led to.

Dreams are hard to chase. They mysteriously guide us through the mystical world of our potential but lack the ability to call out to us in plain language. When our dreams sort of drift away, it can be tempting to let them evaporate. But when we are given an excuse to abandon those dreams, it's time to pause. To think about the future and if we could live with ourselves if we quit—if we stopped the chase and abandoned the hunt for our potential.

The beesting allergy was a perfectly legitimate reason for me to give up on joining the military. But I knew there was still more I could do, and I wouldn't be able to live with myself knowing I had given up so easily. I think my dad knew that the beesting allergy would catch up to me one day. But more importantly, I think he shielded me from quitting too soon on my dream. Medically, the excuse would have been above reproach, but he and I both knew that deep down inside, I never would have been able to accept the end of a dream like that so easily. I couldn't imagine offering the lame excuse that I couldn't join the military because a beesting allergy was the barrier to entry. Holding that single white sheet of paper with those horrible words neatly printed on it should have sealed my fate. I was banned from joining the military through ROTC or any federal service academies. I should have started planning my civilian future. I should have accepted their ruling as final. But I didn't. I refused. I made a few quick Google searches and found hope.

It turned out, some allergies could be cured through an immunization therapy program. These programs were long, usually taking six months for nonsevere allergies. That would disrupt my whole timeline. But there was one small glimmer of hope: There was a shortened version of the therapy a doctor could recommend if they felt the process could be done safely. I needed the shortened version. I called my dad, broke the news to him, and together we made a new plan. I had one more shot to shoot.

A few days later, we drove to Walter Reid National Military Medical Center where a doctor evaluated me. They pricked my skin with six different types of bee and wasp venoms, and I was allergic to them all. A few more tests were run. The doctor went out of the room to analyze the results. My dad and I waited on the edge of our seats. The doctor knocked, came back into the room, and delivered the news:

"Looks like you're a candidate for the immunization therapy program."

One hurdle down, but I didn't have six months. College applications were due in two months. Plus, I still had to get my medical disqualification rescinded and who knew how long that would take. Days mattered.

"What about the rush program?" I asked. Six months of shots across all six venoms in just three days.

He wasn't expecting that request. But he thought about it, discussed it with us, and agreed to allow me to do it. One conversation kept the door to my future open.

The next three days were all the same. Drive to the hospital. Take the elevator up to the third floor. Wave to the lady working behind the front desk. Walk into the third door from the left into a big baby-blue room with three specially designed chairs—the type that you give blood in—and wait to spend the next six hours getting shots every forty-five minutes.

On the second day of the treatment, my stepmom had to leave the room because she didn't want me to see her cry as the staff deliberated

CHAPTER 2

whether they should start injecting my legs because my arms were too swollen and useless to take the shots. At the end of the third day, I received the final injection, along with the mandate to get three shots once a month for the next four years of my life. I had injected my way into immunity.

At Walter Reed, I saw men and women overcoming medical problems far more severe than an allergy. They were getting pricked like pincushions and given shots that were required to save their lives, not enhance immunity to a bee. Some of them did it alone, without the support of their family. Seeing their true heroism was the slap in my face I needed to get out of the self-pity party I had been throwing for myself. I wanted to thank the older generation of warriors for their sacrifice through my future service. If I wanted to be like the heroes around me, I had to find a hero's strength within me. I may be getting crushed with EMT work and losing the opportunity to go to West Point, but at least I had all of my limbs. At least the people I had seen die weren't my friends. Spending time at Walter Reed recalibrated my mindset by showing how much worse things could be.

Time moved on. Later that fall, I completed my college applications and waited for the acceptance letters to start coming in. I was accepted into a school that would guarantee that I would be commissioned into the active duty Army. The rest of senior year went by in a flash, and before I knew it, it was time to leave home and start a new chapter in my life.

Little did I know, new starts without closing the chapter you're in are just another way to run away.

CHAPTER 3

IF YOU ARE DISTRESSED BY ANYTHING EXTERNAL, THE PAIN IS NOT DUE TO THE THING ITSELF, BUT TO YOUR ESTIMATE OF IT; AND THIS YOU HAVE THE POWER TO REVOKE AT ANY MOMENT.

—MARCUS AURELIUS

Like most eighteen-year-olds, I wanted college to be a new start. I chose a university in a completely new state where no one else from my high school was going. But I was also committed to joining the Army and happy to take the first step in my four-year journey to commissioning. I was laser-focused on doing what it took to stay in school and compete for commissioning into the infantry.

Bruising two-a-days kicked off my freshman year as a varsity athlete on the rugby team. The team had a reputation for being tough, and it was true. I also loved foreign languages and cultures, so I learned French and Spanish. But it was the Corps of Cadets requirements that took a busy schedule and turned it into a discipline-forming experience. The Corp of Cadets was separate from ROTC but a mandatory requirement for my university. In the Corps, students formed a makeshift military rank structure with seniors at the top as officer ranks and freshmen at the bottom as junior enlisted ranks.

I wasn't allowed to be on social media or use my cell phone from

CHAPTER 3

five thirty in the morning to nine at night. My door always had to be open, and at any point an upperclassman could come into my room for an impromptu inspection. Beds were made with hospital corners. Uniforms were ironed, folded and stored in certain ways. Dust was the enemy, and it settled in all of the places only the upperclassmen knew where to look. Sharing a room with three other freshmen eliminated any sense of privacy among us. And in that first year, I lost thirty pounds as a freshman, dropping from 210 pounds to 178 at my lowest. My hair was cut so close to my scalp that it might as well have been shaved.

As soon as Thanksgiving break came that year, I found that the difference between me and my old high-school friends was stark. I went to a party with some of my high-school friends and listened as they swapped stories. One of my friends was pledging in a Southern fraternity and had all kinds of wild adventures that made the movies we had seen about college seem like children's stories. Another friend talked about his international love interests as the foreign athlete recruits at his school for some reason found him attractive enough to want to date him. I had nothing to compare with them: no wild parties, no new girlfriend, no skipping classes, and no watching college football in big stadiums. To say my life was different from my friends back home would be an understatement. But I had wanted a harsher college experience. I didn't want to cut loose and party away my college years. I wanted a defining challenge to overcome—probably because I hadn't yet overcome the challenge of EMT work.

After the party, we drove to a nearby 7-Eleven to get some food. As soon as I walked into the store, I saw Lou. It had only been four months since I had stopped volunteering, but it had felt like a lifetime to me. College didn't leave any time to join a volunteer fire department. And anyway, I wasn't in college to pursue a career in emergency medical services. I was there to learn how to become an infantry officer. My high school years had been my last as a first responder to medical emergencies. Or so I told myself.

"Hey, Lou! How's it going?" I asked, hoping for a quick conversation.

I felt like a kid getting caught sneaking into the house after curfew.

"It's good to see you," he replied. "Wait here. Diana and Shannon are in the car; I'll go grab them. They'll want to say hi."

I was a deer caught in the headlights. Nothing about the encounter was awkward, but the paralyzing fear inside of me made me want to run out of the store. I didn't want to see them. I didn't want to see my firehouse family. This was supposed to be a clandestine homecoming without any of the reminders of what had made me want to leave it in the first place. But Lou didn't know that. My ongoing mistake was that I never let my teammates know I wasn't doing well.

"How is college?" Diana asked. She and Lou stood on either side of their daughter, each holding one of her hands, all three smiling at me.

"It's going pretty well. I'm home on Thanksgiving break," I said. "You're getting older," I told Shannan.

"Are you coming to the meeting on Friday? We have to pay our dues for the upcoming year if you want to stay active," Lou said.

Dues. How strange—I had paid for the privilege of volunteering my high school years away. I had paid for the right to be a member of the fire department. I had paid to be so worn down. I had been all in. But I didn't feel all in anymore. I couldn't spend another second in the fire department, let alone spend any money on it. I could even spare the time to think about it. I was in full flight mode.

"Yeah, I'll be there," I said.

Lou knew I wouldn't show. For the first time, I think he saw through the lies I had been telling him for the past two years. I had only ever been saying what I thought tough men expected to hear. I'll never forget the look he gave me. He paused at the door while he left the store and looked back at me, standing in line still waiting to cash out. It seemed like he wanted to say something. But he didn't. He threw a casual wave goodbye, and, like a true cowboy, he didn't look back.

I had hoped choosing a college away from my hometown would let me move on. But I had found I couldn't escape myself.

After my academic freshman year, I studied at the Republic of

CHAPTER 3

Moldova's Military Academy for a month and took the rest of summer break at my family's cabin in Maine. Stripped of simple luxuries like electricity and running water, I found a freedom in releasing societal comforts.

With no one else around to correct my undomesticated behavior, I turned into a feral sort of creature. I grew a beard in rebellion against the military grooming standards that ruled my life as a student. Showers happened when I jumped into the lake after a workout. I wore a two-week-old dip-spit stain on a campfire-scented hoodie, and all other laundry happened when I hopped into the lake with my dirty clothes on and then hung them up to dry in the wind.

A good day was waking up with the sunrise and walking down to the lake, when the water was as still and smooth as glass and a loon would call out across the loneliness of the water. A cup of coffee and a breakfast cooked on a cast-iron skillet over a wood fire was bliss—unlike the way cooking and cleaning feels like work in a kitchen. Reading was my only form of entertainment, and I devoured the books I'd brought with me. I read Palo Cuellar, Louis L'Amour, Lt. Col. Dave Grossman, and Conn Iggulden. The days ended after a workout in the afternoon and watching the sunset drop off the western end of the lake.

Living was simple. I had almost forgotten what it was I had gone there to run from. But it found me again. After three weeks of total isolation at the lake, a classmate who also lived in Maine came to visit before we headed back for the start of rugby camp in early August. But before we left, we had a fun few days fishing, kayaking, shooting rifles, and cooking over an open fire.

The drive down South took us down Interstate 95—a beautiful, albeit boring, highway. I had been in the woods so long that even listening to music felt strange and somehow indulgent. Only one Canadian radio station had floated in and out at camp, getting especially weak and unreadable whenever it was cloudy. My senses had for the first time in my life calibrated to almost no external stimulus. I had been left alone with my thoughts for weeks, devoid of any external input.

I was enjoying the luxury of music and trying not to worry about my impending return to life when my friend yelled from the passenger seat, "Pull over!"

His outburst jolted me from the daze of a four-hour road trip.

"Pull over!" he said again, pointing toward the shoulder of the off-ramp. He still didn't have any words to explain the situation to me.

I had been in my own world, focused on changing lanes and merging off the highway. But my friend had just watched a motorcycle slam unceremoniously into a guard rail at forty miles an hour in the oncoming lane.

"What's wrong?" I demanded, pulling over even though I hadn't seen or heard the wreck. Did I have a flat tire? Was my engine smoking?

"That guy just crashed!" he said, jerking a thumb behind us and to the left.

My mind instantly cleared, and the familiar sensation of the hero's drug started pumping through my veins. I put on my flashers and checked the side mirror before opening up my door next to oncoming traffic.

"Call 911!" I told my friend as we ran toward the biker. He had cartwheeled off the bike, which had shattered against the metal guardrail that was the only thing preventing him from falling down the steep side of a hill. His blue jeans were shredded and smeared red with blood. His sweatshirt had done little to protect against the sanding effect of asphalt abrading his skin. Thankfully, his cracked and broken helmet had acted as the substitute for what undoubtedly would have been his shattered skull. One of his legs was broken at the femur. Bone jutted through skin and bulged underneath his jeans, and his broken leg was noticeably shorter than the other.

"My leg!" screamed the man. "It hurts!"

"Call 911!" I repeated to my friend. His phone was in his hand, but he hadn't made the call. He was looking at the man. Frozen. Adrenaline.

"Call 911 and tell them where we are. I'm going to take care of him. Get the call through!" I said again.

"Straighten out my leg!" the man screamed at me. He was rolling

CHAPTER 3

around on the road, clutching at his disfigured limb.

There was no way I was going to try to set his femur on the spot. It required a splint that used gears to generate enough power to pull traction. If I tried to move his leg, the sharp as knives bone shards could cut his femoral artery and he would bleed out in a matter of seconds. I checked the blood pooling under his jeans, hoping it wasn't an arterial bleed already. I took off my belt, ready to make a hasty tourniquet if needed. After a moment, I could tell it was just regular bleeding because his skin was broken where the bone protruded.

My friend finished getting help to our location while I began triage. Based on the mechanism of injury—the crash—the man could have any number of injuries. But in a crisis, we fall back on training. And the training I had received as an EMT provided order out of the chaos. Is he breathing? He was talking to me. That required air, so I moved to the next item. How bad is he bleeding? I checked his leg one more time then started swiping my hands across his back, pulling them out after each pass to see if he was bleeding from anywhere else. Next I needed a baseline of his vitals so I could tell if his condition was deteriorating. I grabbed his wrist and counted his pulse for fifteen seconds, multiplying that number by four. I also couldn't hear any rasping noises or signs of distressed breathing, which was a good sign. For the moment, he was conscious and aware of his surroundings.

The man reached up and pulled off his helmet as he continued to roll around, his broken leg flopping along with each turn. His head and neck looked good. His arms were raw and bleeding but didn't look broken. My attention could stay focused on his leg.

"Hey man," I said, putting my hand on his chest to gently keep him from rolling in pain. "You're doing great. Help is on its way."

"I can't believe I wrecked," he said. His pale face contorted in pain, contrasting his dark brown beard.

Maine can be a small place, even in the more populated southern part of the state. As fate would have it, a family member of his was a nurse and had been passing by on her way home from the local hospital. The traffic around us rubbernecked, and when she recognized him, she pulled over to help. She consoled him as he went into shock. He started to squirm less. He stared off blankly into the distance. He stopped asking me to straighten out his leg. Soon after, the EMTs arrived and took the man away. His sister followed. And we left.

Back in my car, the old feelings from high-school EMT work resurfaced. Faces of calls from the past trickled into my mind. I wondered how they were. I had been so inoculated to the usual end of a call that I didn't even recognize an opportunity to get healthy closure on an event like that. I could have asked for her number. I could have followed up on the man with the broken femur. Instead of finding proper closure for the emergency in that moment, a different call pushed itself to the forefront of my mind. It was a different motorcycle accident, and it had happened in the spring of my senior year of high school.

I had just turned eighteen a few weeks before and was really feeling the weight of my perceived failures. I came into the station early that Saturday, feeling like I needed a win. A big win. I needed to save someone's life to offset the lives I hadn't been able to save so far. Like normal, the radio set off the alarm, and we grabbed our gear and took off in the ambulance, Lou driving and Jon riding shotgun.

We were the second crew to arrive on scene. A motorcycle was crumpled underneath the rear wheels of an SUV. The speed limit for the road was 50 mph, a devastating speed for a motorcycle collision. The first crew surrounded a body, working furiously to save him. He was backboarded, neck-braced, and nearly ready to be loaded into the back of the ambulance. Little attention was being given to a teenage boy nearby.

My patient was the boy.

"How are you doing, boss?" I asked, kneeling on the hard asphalt next to him, carefully avoiding the broken shards of glass and plastic that littered the scene.

"I'm okay," he lied. "How's my dad?"

"I'm not too sure. I'll update you when I hear something. How about I take a look at you?" I said as calmly as I could.

CHAPTER 3

The kid was bleeding from his head and his pupils were dilated, indicating brain injury. There was a baseball-sized welt on top of his arm where the bone was broken. All over his body, there were streaks of blood and patches of burned-off skin from where the momentum of the crash had dragged his body along the road. His wounds seeped blood the way a popped blister weeps out puss.

Head wounds bleed a lot and can look more severe than they really are, but because of the mechanism of the injury (the motorcycle crash) he could have been suffering from a fractured skull, broken neck, broken back, concussion, and a whole list of internal injuries. I treated him for the worst. Better to play it safe, I thought as I prepared bandages, a neck brace, and the backboard.

"Tell me what happened," I said as I measured and carefully put the neck brace on him without disturbing his neck or back.

"We were riding. I was on the back and my dad was driving the motorcycle. He pulled out and didn't see the SUV change lanes into his turn. The SUV hit us. I flew through the side window and came out the back window. I don't know what happened to my dad. You have to tell me what happened to my dad," he pleaded.

I prepared a splint for his arm. And wrapped his head in a white bandage, stopping the flow of red streaming onto his face.

The first crew took off, their lights and sirens wailing their way toward Shock Trauma, the highest form of medical care we could get him. It was a matter of life and death. We backboarded the teenager before picking him up and placing him on the stretcher. We rolled him to the back of the ambulance, loaded him in, and were on our way.

We flew down the highway as fast as we could. The kid was stable, but we had no idea what was happening internally. No one should have survived the crash he had just experienced. It was a twenty-minute ride to the hospital, and throughout the whole ride he only asked one question. Not for water, not to be placed in a more comfortable position, not for his neck brace to be adjusted. He only asked about his dad.

When we wheeled him into Shock Trauma and their team took over, it was the most professional environment I had ever seen—and a wonder of modern science. My job was downgraded to pushing the stretcher into the elevator and up to the emergency room. The room was massive. It smelled clean and was illuminated by a bright white light. We wheeled the boy to an open bed, separated from the others by a hanging curtain that could be drawn into the middle of the big room, providing a tiny bit of privacy for each patient. His father was two beds to his right. We heard machines beep and turn on. Shouted orders echoed, and the room was alive with activity. One machine sounded like a saw. I could only imagine what was happening.

As we walked away, I heard the son ask about his father one more time.

It struck me that he wasn't just a son asking about his dad. He was a boy asking about his hero. His dad had been teaching him how to drive a motorcycle. It was probably how they bonded. Most likely, they were on one of the last rides before he would get his own bike and they could ride together. Now he was listening to his father fight for his life two beds away while he suffered silently in his own personal hell. I have no idea if the father lived, but if I had to place a bet, I'd say he didn't. I have no idea if the son ever rode a motorcycle again. Everything I know about their story ended when I walked out of Shock Trauma and took the ambulance back to the firehouse.

My heart went out to the boy, but I never heard from him again. That afternoon in Maine, before my friend and I got back into the car to finish the drive, I could have asked the family member for her number. I could have called her a day later and asked how he was doing, if he kept his leg, what his recovery timeline would be. I could have known if I had done a good job. But every call before then had ended the same way. There was never a period at the end of the story; my role in the call ceased and with that all access to the patient went as well. There were no happy endings under this model.

Every time I left a call without knowing if one of my patients lived

CHAPTER 3

had created a story in my mind that had no ending. There was no closure. All I had was the worst parts of the call replaying themselves in my mind as if that was the only thing that had happened to the person. I never saw their recovery, and it was as if I never learned how to recover either.

When we finished the road trip to my friend's house, we parted ways.

"That was crazy," my friend said.

"Yeah, man. That was wild," I said.

"I hope he's okay," he said later, as we said our goodbyes.

I don't remember ever talking about the crash again with my friend. It would have been natural to tell his father, who was a policeman, but I am not sure we even did that much. Between the two of us, we sort of just forgot about the whole thing.

It's natural to view our present through the lens of our past. But what that does is it creates a mode of living where we stop growing. We only see reality the way that it once appeared to us. Our bodies can age, but our souls don't move on. Wherever you are right now, you might not know if you are locked in survival mode without closure. How could you? It could even be that the only mode of existence you have ever known is survival. But if you've just "sort of forgotten" without seeking closure, you could be robbing yourself without even knowing that you are the thief of your own happiness. I learned another lesson after that crash: I learned that I could avoid but I couldn't forget.

At barely twenty years old I had to confront that life happens unexpectedly. I had gone into the Maine wilderness looking for an escape, looking for an adventure that was nothing like the life I had lived as a high schooler and a freshman in college. Perhaps I instinctively knew I needed to heal—that I had built a habit of avoiding pain—in the same way that someone realizes they are starting to drink too much during the workweek to get rid of stress.

When I went into the woods, I went away from civilization as best as I could manage. I wanted to learn the metrics of a day well-lived, of a life well-lived, and the peace that can come and rest upon us when we don't have all the pressure of the world crashing down on us via social media and the internet. I needed the calm that nature could provide because inside I was in constant turmoil. I was constantly at a boil when the rest of the world wasn't even simmering. I could fly off the handle in a rage because of things that didn't faze other people. I had emerged from solitude only to experience the crash immediately afterward, and I felt myself slip back into old familiar habits. Avoidance. Shame. Ruthless self-talk. They all came back, and I greeted them like old friends, not as the enemy they really were.

The sense of aloneness and survival-focused behavior that unresolved trauma causes magnifies the impact painful events have in our lives. In a sense, we suffer exponentially more in our own minds after the event. We lose our sense of time, forgetting that the painful moment is not happening in the present. We relive each moment in the past with the same intensity in our present. We remember with the stark clarity of a movie the scenes, faces, characters, sights and smells. They attach themselves to us and distort each new experience we have with the clouded judgment of the past.

When life hurts us, it's natural to act like a wounded animal and seek out some place of solitude where we can lick our wounds. We close ourselves off and say we will never love again after we lose a relationship. We get burned in business and say that we will never trust another partner or employer. We watch our parents' divorce and say that lasting love doesn't exist. Licking our wounds is a form of self-medicating. Sometimes that turns to alcohol, drugs, and relationships to give us any sense of positive emotions. But pain is compounded when we think that the only way to endure it is silently and on our own.

When you think about your life, are there memories that haunt you? Are there experiences you still don't have words to describe? Have you experienced pain so deep and unsettling that you not only try to hide from it, but you hide it from others as well? Do you feel like no one else could possibly understand what you have been through? Do you feel alone in the wilderness?

If we don't learn to look our pain in the face and recognize it not

CHAPTER 3

as the single most defining aspect of our lives but simply as a chapter in our life story, we will remain under its thumb. Trapped and helpless. Small and scared. We only give ourselves the three options we have when we face a predator: fight, flight, or freeze. We focus on survival, identifying threats, and preserving whatever sense of security we can find.

Without pausing to see our pain for what it is and to learn about ourselves in light of it, we can live a lot of life as strangers in our own bodies. It's not that we should publicly air our dirty laundry to the world, or that we should seek out self-serving attention to fill a void in our hearts. But we can't stay isolated, either. We ought to look to the examples of people who have similar struggles to our own and model ourselves after them. To learn how to stop running. How to stop fighting those around us who aren't our enemies. To learn how to live from those who don't seek escape or disappear into loops of the past. To experience each moment as it comes.

When you are young, the only lens you have to view suffering through is your own. Most of the experiences that hurt you when you are younger are happening to you for the first time, so you don't have a framework to defend against them. You don't have the experience of successfully negotiating that obstacle. When it looms in front of you, you approach it with the perspective that you have always had. That's youth. It's naivete and bravery and hope all bundled together, waiting to be dashed to pieces by forces outside your control. And it will—because life isn't fair.

I think Lou knew that. I raged at the injustice of a boy watching and listening to his dad die in the room next to him. I raged at the injustice of never knowing if anything I was doing on other people's behalf made any difference. I wanted control where it felt like I had none. But the things I tried to control were never going to be within my power. I wanted to control the outcome instead of focusing on my effort. I wanted to control a stable source of love instead of my ability to love others as generously and authentically as I could. I wanted to control the quiet voice in my head that told me I didn't deserve happiness.

Seeing something wrong and trying to fix it is an authentic impulse to build yourself into a "hero"—to become the kind of person who can do something about that issue. But it's no small thing to change the world, and very little is actually within your control. If you aren't prepared, the world will change you. And the love and compassion that set you on your journey will be the first internal casualties.

Yet, whatever the circumstances of your life may be, if you can pause in the present, you'll always find something within your power. Spend a morning drinking coffee and watching the sunrise, and maybe you will feel something that you never have before. Maybe you will get a glimmer of peace. You will feel what it is to release the outcome of a situation or relationship and to just show up to life.

It took lying to Lou for me to realize I was in flight mode. I thought that I was in some way stronger for not looking back. In reality, the unclosed chapter of my EMT work was locking me in place as the same EMT kid I had been so many months before. I wasn't growing as I got older; I was trapped in the same mind with a different body, hoping no one would notice.

What I really needed to face was that, at some point in my EMT career, I had stopped doing it for other people. When I'd first started out, I was happy responding to any call, no matter how trivial or unimportant it seemed. At the end of my EMT career, I would be angry if I didn't respond to a life-or-death medical emergency or disturbing traumatic injury. Each call was a hopeful scenario where I could replay old failed calls and get a new chance to save someone else. Really what I wanted was more opportunities to save myself.

Looking back on that conversation in 7-Eleven with Lou, I should have told the truth.

I should have said, "Hey Lou, it's great to see you."

He would have replied the same, "It's good to see you too. Are you coming to the meeting on Friday?"

Maybe it would have taken more courage than an eighteen-year-old should be expected to have, but I should have taken a breath. I

CHAPTER 3

should have looked him in the eyes and said, "Lou I'm not going to be there. I'm tired. I'm not sure I can keep doing EMT work."

I don't know what he would have said after that. But I think he would have known what I meant. I think he would recognize the fatigue of a soul locked in a fight with itself. I think he would understand that I was running from all of the calls that didn't go our way, and I think he would have thought more of me instead of less of me. Instead I kept myself trapped in my code of silence. I bought into the lie that looking like everything was under control mattered more than being at peace. I worried that if my walls came down, then there would be nothing left to keep me safe. It's a trap that many of us experience. The walls we build when we are young become the ramparts we use to block intimacy and healing when we are adults.

If I had told him the truth and opened myself up to the magic of honest dialogue, maybe he would have offered to go grab a beer at some dark bar where the glasses stick to the bar table and waitresses don't ask for IDs before they serve a beer. Maybe he could have told me how he worked through the calls that didn't sit well with him. Maybe I could have learned how to be a man, struggling to grapple with the suffering that life imposes on the people who are the least capable of resisting it. I could have seen the image of the rough and tumble cowboy lift—a glimpse of humanity, shocked by the horror of blood and disfigured limbs. I could have seen compassion as a strength, not the weakness I learned to loathe it as.

In many ways, that moment in 7-Eleven was when and where healing could have begun for me. Instead, it was just another moment where I lied to myself and to a man who didn't deserve to be lied to. I lied to a teammate, and later on I would have teammates lie to me. And the consequences of both were tragic in every sense of the word.

CHAPTER 4

ALL THE GODS, ALL THE HEAVENS, ALL THE HELLS, ARE WITHIN YOU.

—JOSEPH CAMPBELL

Before my summer in the woods the summer after my freshman year, I went to the Republic of Moldova's military academy for a month-long language and cultural immersion trip. Moldova is a beautiful place that is old in the way that the United States is young. It has a history of warfare and conflict, oppression and struggle. It has been fought over by empires, swallowed by larger neighbors, and even had a civil war in the 1990s, yet it's maintained its own identity. The men there are as tough as generational-inspired freedom fighters can be.

Being in a foreign place is like dating a new person. At first just the thought, sight, and smells of the new country are intoxicating. Doing anything in your new land is exciting. Adventure masks even the mundane. But like a budding romance, at some point the love affair loses its novelty—most likely when you realize how hard it is to communicate without knowing the local language.

Just going to the store is uncannily difficult in a foreign country. You have to figure out what time the store is open and then how to get there. You have to decide what brands to get or even the type of

CHAPTER 4

food you're looking at. You have to figure out if you can pay with a credit card or if you need to pay in cash and what the price is in your new currency. Worst of all, you have to face the cashier. Someone who doesn't speak your language, nor you theirs, and then you have to reach them at a level deeper than words can communicate. The cashier sees the bread and knows why you are in the store, so that's not a difficult concept to communicate with gestures and looks. And when you place money on the counter, the interaction is complete. Maybe you try to be polite and say the one phrase you remembered in their language and thank them, but for the most part, the stress of the moment is over. You leave the store and walk out onto the street, soon to be confronted with your next challenge.

I loved it. I had to trust myself to communicate with more than words and realized that I could survive with a primal sort of communication that exists among all of us. I learned to get my needs met without language at all.

I met a Moldovan friend on that trip. He had buzzed hair and the stone face that Eastern European men all seem to be born with. He was a calisthenics fitness phenom. There were pull-up bars outside of their barracks where he would do muscle-up after muscle-up. He could flip and invert himself under or over the bar in insane displays of core strength. He could plank, he could dip, he could hang with one hand, he could spin and catch himself in the middle of a pull-up . . . Naturally, when I started working out next to him, I knew I couldn't compete with his skills. I could do twenty pull-ups in a row. He did more. And not only could he do more but he could do more reps each consecutive set after me. The pull-up bar was fundamentally his domain of expertise.

We both spoke French and while we waited between sets, we would have conversations in that shared language. My Moldovan friend and I talked about our families. His dad was in the Soviet Army and had fought in Afghanistan in the 1980s. He said that the war changed his dad. Afterward, he drank more, and when he drank, it made him violent. Strangely, my father had been in the United States Army in the 1980s. In the Cold War era, our fathers were enemies. Trained to kill each other—because that's what soldiers are trained to do. Just one generation later, the sons of enemies had become friends. Even weirder, if we had both lived thirty years earlier, we would have been enemies.

A similar connection was forged when we visited a World War II war memorial on one of our outings, and a man who could have been any of our grandfathers led the tour. The memorial was at a point on the western side of the Dniester River that flowed between the Republic of Moldova, a breakaway region called Transdniestria, and Ukraine. The man giving the tour had escaped ahead of the German Army. He found his way into the Soviet Red Army and was a part of the enormous human suffering that was the Eastern Front.

For the Moldovan veteran, WWII wasn't a war to liberate a continent—it was a war to save his family and liberate his home. The fighting happened near his home village. He saw the destruction war unleashes when it passes through a place, except he knew the place well. It was the place he was standing on as he talked to us. It had been his home. He pointed across the river banks as he talked about the combat he endured. It was a contested water crossing, which is one of the worst offensive missions to have. German artillery fired on them from the western side of the river bank as they prepared to cross. Machine gunners poured their bullets into the engineers who crafted a pontoon bridge. German riflemen fired well-aimed shots and killed the Soviet infantrymen who charged their way through steel and lead over the Dniester.

The old man was crumpled and sagging with the weight of old age on his shoulders. In his fighting years, I bet he drank vodka like a fish and smoked cigarettes like a chimney. But overlooking the battlefield of his youth and the land that has been contested by empires and governments for a thousand years, he teared up. Our translator struggled to find the words in English that mirrored what the man was saying, but we got the point. He was thinking about his friends, maybe

CHAPTER 4

some of whom died within sight of where we were standing.

If he had been American, he would have worn a blue hat embroidered in the gold lettering of the VFW. In that moment, I think he was a veteran hero and a grandfather to all of us. He was the manifestation of the archetypical warrior from an older generation forever changed by war when his youth was stolen from him by forces outside his control. He told us that he visited his village after the offensive had ended—he went home. Only I wondered if he ever really came home after all the fighting was done.

Maybe a part of him was still out there on the far side of the bank. Still fighting. Still wondering if he was going to die. Still horrified at the sights and sounds and smells that happened all at once as he saw his friends die around him in a land that had been filled with happy memories of his childhood. What memories won out inside his soul?

When he was done talking, and after we had thanked him for his time, the old man stood with his cane and walked away from the memorial, having said his piece. And for him, in that moment, it looked like it was enough.

When we live authentically we become living symbols for things much greater than ourselves. It's almost like we embody a deeper sense of truth by our actions. The old Moldovan warrior lived out a truth to the future warriors of a nation that had once been a declared enemy. Truth transcends cultures. It connects hearts that languages cannot break through.

I found another truth in words written in my own language by an old warrior who again found me in Moldova. It happened unexpectedly one Sunday morning while I was reading during some free time. Our barracks were just a big room where boys slept on one side in an endless row of cots, and the female cadets slept on the other side. At the end of the room, opposite the doorway, there was a box full of English language books that the Moldovan military academy had provided us, no doubt from their English department. The first book I picked up was called *Tears of a Warrior,* written by a Vietnam veteran and his wife.

I was intrigued right away. The author had been severely wounded and discharged from the Army. His war-torn body healed, but his war-weary soul didn't. And his family suffered because of it. PTSD gripped him, strangling away the happiness and love his family could have provided him. The book was his story of survival and recovery, but I read his words as if they were describing me. Without ever having put a label on myself, I read the signs of PTSD as if it were the normal operating system that every young person was encoded with. For years that had been the lens through which I viewed the world, and this book was the first time I was told I could find a new lens.

The timing of the book was impeccable. I had just spent a month struggling to communicate with my new friends in a foreign country. But I learned a new foreign language because of the book—the language of compassion. Both his compassion for others like him and the compassion I could have for myself. For the first time in my life, I had a way to articulate the true depths of pain, the level of confusion, and the frustration I had felt for so long.

Two years later, after my junior year of college, I studied at a language school in the foothills of the French Alps—the culminating adventure of my university experience. In class, I sat next to a monk. A real-life monk, he was in his midthirties and had a long black goatee with close-cropped hair. He wore sandals, cargo shorts, and a T-shirt. He spoke English with a Polish accent. French with a Spanish accent. But the man had a language unto his own. He could reach you on a soul level, in a way that constantly surprised me.

Grenoble was home to the famous author Stendhal. I hadn't read any of his books yet, and when I walked past his house on a tour, I didn't notice anything remarkable about the stone building pointed out to me. What I did notice were the bars nearby. And so did my friend the monk. We waited patiently for class to be over in typical French fashion, which was early, and then grabbed a table at a bar. After enough beers, we began to philosophize. He knew about stoicism, having read the masterworks of philosophy in Latin while he was a

CHAPTER 4

student at the Vatican. It seemed like he broke philosophy into one language and religion into another. He was fluent in both, and they even seemed related to each other, in the way Spanish and Italian are similar. I didn't know Latin and I didn't know about stoicism. He patiently fielded my questions, including how one could be religious and still maintain a personal philosophy.

"Do you fast?" I asked.

"Yes, I fast and I pray on some holidays. On other holidays the brothers and I drink beer and eat good food."

"What is life like in a monastery?" I asked.

"We wake up early, we pray, we eat, we work, we pray, we work again, we eat again, and we pray again. Then we sleep. That is my life. The monastery is simple," he said.

"Don't you miss this?" I asked, gesturing to the bustling bar around me. "Don't you miss being connected to the world?"

Our conversation was interrupted when two of our classmates found us and asked if they could join us. They were both from South America and spoke Spanish. The monk and I also spoke Spanish, so we ordered cervezas and practiced Spanish with our friends.

Our Columbian friend was edgy, a lip and nose ring added to the mystique that her dark eyes, dirty-blond hair, and dark skin already emitted. Tattoos peeked out from her trendy clothes when she moved. The monk puzzled me. How could he look at her beauty, or the beauty of any woman, and not be attracted to her? Or if he was attracted to her, what did he do when he felt that emotion?

Our second friend was from Chile and was gay. He wore leather bracelets and a chic drooping necklace. He rolled his own cigarettes and would always offer me one during lunch breaks. I would always decline, not confident in my ability to take a drag without coughing, and this guy was too cool to embarrass myself in front of. He had a way of looking at people sideways, and he had a ruthless wit. No doubt the monk would disapprove. But here we were. Drinking beer together. Talking. Learning about each other's lives and learning each other's plans for the future.

What I didn't realize was that this monk was on his heroic journey too, even though it wasn't the path I would have chosen in a million years. But he was on it. He was happy. The sense of fulfillment I received by chasing my dream to join the military was the same joy he received for pursuing his purpose. He followed his code of ethics, as best I could tell, without becoming either a prude or descending into depravity at the first opportunity to taste freedom. He was in the zone. He could connect with us while remaining true to himself. He was surrounded by people utterly different from himself, yet he was at peace. He withheld judgments. He showed me what living a principled life connected to other people could look like. He had a way of looking into people's souls and making them feel seen.

I should have ordered another beer, waited for our friends to leave, and soaked in more wisdom the monk had to offer. I should have asked him to explain stoicism to me more. I should have asked him to lay it out to me line by line. Book by book. Philosopher by philosopher. But instead of sticking around, I paid my tab and went out to meet some other friends at a club.

When I woke up the next morning, I sipped water and nibbled at a baguette to cure my hangover while I googled "stoicism." I wanted to learn more about it as a philosophy. Who started it? What were the rules I had to follow if I wanted to practice it in my own life?

I read that stoicism began in ancient Greece by a man named Zeno. He famously taught his students on a porch, or stoa—how the term stoicism began—in a way that met a need that religion had yet to provide the ancient Greeks. Ancient minds were hungry for explanations of the world, but ancient religion encouraged superstition. When life caused people to suffer, the answer was to pray and sacrifice in order to find favor in the eyes of the gods. Stoicism challenged the belief that human beings were divine playthings. If humans could learn to control their minds, they could become indifferent to the suffering inflicted on them by fate.

Stoicism is traditionally viewed in three phases. The first phase was the Greek founding. The second phase marks the transition from Greece to Rome as the seat of stoic philosophy, though much of the stoic work composed by this period of philosophers has been lost to history. The third phase is the Roman period, which many Renaissance and Enlightenment thinkers relied upon as tenets of that philosophy. From this period, Seneca, Marcus Aurelius, and Epictetus emerged.

The first philosopher, Seneca, lived from around 4 BC to 65 AD He had vast wealth and influence within the Roman government while serving as an adviser to Emperor Nero. A useful collection of his thoughts and wisdom is preserved in letters are found in the *Tao of Seneca*, which organizes his writings into topics like anger, the shortness of life, and suffering. He provides deep insight into what stoicism meant in the ancient world, and many examples he gives on how to live a stoic life are still applicable to modern times.

The second philosopher, Emperor Marcus Aurelius, lived from around AD 121 to AD 180. He was the most powerful man in the world during his lifetime. As emperor, he could have anything and anyone he wanted. He was the kind of leader who had absolute power and the ruthless societal standards that allowed him to use any means necessary to get what he wanted. But instead of using power as a means to accumulate money, women, and glory, he chose to live a controlled and temperate life. He dutifully fulfilled the responsibilities of his office. Many of his thoughts and wisdom are preserved in the book *Meditations*, which is a journal of sorts that was never intended for publication. Marcus Aurelius used stoicism as a means to gird himself for the crushing burden of leading a nation during wars, rebellions, and plagues.

The third teacher, Epictetus, lived from AD 55 to AD 135. His life differs significantly from the power, wealth, and influence of the Roman elite. He was a crippled slave. His path to freedom was bought by his ability to educate himself and to become a great teacher. Central to his pathway to liberty was the philosophy of stoicism. He became renowned for his wisdom and taught a body of students who preserved his teachings in written form—*Discourses* and *Enchiridion*. Epictetus lived a cruel and unfair life, yet he taught himself how to live a free life as a slave and as a banished intellectual. He showed modern stoics what an indomitable spirit is capable of. He serves his modern readers from his lived example of overcoming all the odds to make something of himself from nothing.

My life and my friend the monk's life seemed very different. I didn't want rules about what to wear, about what to eat or drink or when to go to sleep. I wanted to live life on my terms. I rejected the idea of people in positions of authority telling me what I should or shouldn't do. Perhaps I wasn't not so different from teenagers at that age after all.

While technology has changed, the human soul remains closely linked to our ancient ancestors. I read more and more about stoicism during my time in France. I learned that stoics try to live a virtuous life. And that they use courage, temperance, wisdom, and justice to guide their decision-making. Some rules are good to follow, especially simple ones, like treating others how you would want to be treated. Our actions have consequences, and we can hurt one another and ourselves if we aren't careful. For example, a hangover is a hell of a thing to do to yourself. In the head-throbbing throes of self-induced suffering, we often promise ourselves "never again." But then the next Friday night comes, and we belly up to the bar to order our drinks just the same. The lesson of temperance remains yet to be learned by many young college kids.

One quote from Marcus Aurelius stood out to me: "You have power over your mind—not outside events. Realize this, and you will find strength." I didn't feel like I had power over my mind. And to be honest, I didn't understand what that meant anyway. How would I take control of my mind? My limited language and understanding had boxed me into a judgment of the monk and, ultimately, myself. I mistakenly believed there were two options: a life of rules or a life of freedom. Clearly, there was an element of enlightenment I was still unaware of.

CHAPTER 5

THE STRENGTH OF A PERSON'S SPIRIT WOULD THEN BE MEASURED BY HOW MUCH "TRUTH" HE COULD TOLERATE.

—FREIDRICH NIETZSCHE

After France, I coasted into my last semester of college with a simple academic roster, taking all the soft electives I needed to round out my bachelor of arts degree. Philosophy was one, with a "crunchy" granola-type professor who liked to skateboard and wouldn't drink coffee for one month of the year just to prove to himself that he didn't have a caffeine addiction. Naturally, he taught the class about stoicism. There, I read the passages from Seneca, Epictetus, and Marcus Aurelius that had turned up in my Google search. Stoicism didn't take hold of me or convert me the way you'd kneel at the altar on a Sunday morning. But I guess a philosophy that had lasted two thousand years wasn't in a hurry to break into my world. It could wait. And so could I.

In the spring, I was commissioned into the Infantry. The unit I was going to was stationed near the Canadian border. After graduation and commissioning, I crammed all of my worldly possessions into my 2005 Honda Civic and drove down to Georgia to move into my own apartment. For the next ten weeks, I had one mission: pass the

Infantry Basic Officer Leader Course (IBOLC) and earn my blue cord (the mark of every US Army infantryman). After that, Ranger School.

United States Army Ranger School—the Army's premier light infantry tactics school—had been waiting for me since the day I decided I would grow up to join the Army. My father graduated from Ranger School, and I kept a picture of him with his graduating class on my bedside table growing up. Ranger School stories were my bedtime stories. Apparently, the blueberry pancakes in the mountain phase were really good in 1986. Over the years, he brought up other details too. He told me about the winter and mentioned that the cold makes training harder. He talked about the importance of having a Ranger buddy, someone who could look out for you, warm up their feet in your armpits, or nudge you awake on security. He talked about things like droning, when your mind reverts to a sleep-like state, but the body keeps walking, rucking, and moving. He talked about how he craved Snickers dunked in peanut butter and didn't understand why anyone would think that was weird.

When I would ask my dad questions about passing Ranger School, I wanted to know the *how*—my dad wisely stuck to the *what* and *why*. There's no step-by-step instruction manual on how to accomplish a dream, and there's no way to know how to succeed in a place where so much of what happens is outside your control. His stories also lacked the intensity of what he felt as a young lieutenant going through the school. And that makes sense too; time lessens the sting of pain. He wasn't hiding the difficulty from me, but at the same time, I think he knew what was in store for me and wanted to shield me from thinking it would be too hard or difficult. He didn't want to scare me off from chasing a dream that he knew would be the hardest thing I would do in my life—up to that point at least.

After I graduated from IBOLC, the colonel in charge of Ranger School was invited as the guest speaker at a formal dinner, and he took a different tack. He told us that in the middle of a firefight in Afghanistan, as rocket-propelled grenades exploded around him and

CHAPTER 5

bullets snapped past his position, he had the conscious thought that the firefight wasn't as bad as Ranger School. "That," he said, "was the value of Ranger School." You could be in war, but at least you weren't in a Florida swamp in wintertime or shoveling snow in the Georgia mountains to make a fighting position. Things could always be worse, and in war, Ranger School was his mark of how bad things could get. I think he was trying to encourage us, that what we were about to do had a purpose and that it would be worth it if we stuck through the training and made it out on the other side.

There is a debate among Ranger School students about who has it harder: summer students or winter students. Summers in Georgia and Florida are hot, and the heat is a killer. Just one class before I started, a student died from a heat-related injury. Some of the guys I was waiting to start Ranger School with knew him. I decided that it didn't matter what season I went through the school; I couldn't control the weather. But that didn't stop me from doing some weather forecasting when our start dates were given to us. It turned out that if I went straight through, our class would catch the last heat waves of fall and then the first cold fronts of winter. If I recycled, I would be in the full throes of winter by the time I got out. My dad was a winter Ranger, and while there weren't any deaths, he talked about the injuries his platoon sustained. One guy lost three fingers to frostbite. Once, after a week of patrolling, they hadn't slept much and were by a fire getting warm for the first time that whole week. A guy fell asleep standing up and toppled over into the flames. They put him out before he was too burned to keep training.

Ranger School consists of four phases. The first is called the Ranger Assessment Phase. Across four days, students complete a fitness test, a combat water survival assessment, a night- and day-land-navigation test, an obstacle course, and a twelve-mile ruck. Phase Two teaches the fundamentals of squad-level ambushes and reconnaissance missions. Phase Three teaches platoon-level patrolling in the mountains of northwest Georgia. Phase Four is the "jungle" or swamp phase, conducted in Florida. Throughout all the phases, combat conditions are simulated by limiting students' food and sleep and increasing their exposure to nature's elements.

We had our share of injuries. There are two obstacle courses called Malvesti and Darby Queen, and on Darby Queen you climb a rope up to a balance beam suspended thirty feet in the air. The guy in front of me biffed it off the top and shattered his leg when his fall stopped thirty feet below. Ranger instructors dragged him to the side while medics were called to treat him. I knew the guy, and five months later when I saw him again, he was getting out of the Army because his leg was obliterated so badly. I contracted cellulitis in my right knee, which turned a hot puffy red and hurt when I extended my leg to walk. At night we would wear night-vision goggles that turn the blackness of night into shades of green. That light plays havoc with your mind when you haven't slept in days and are walking up mountains. Once, a green goblin with a hooked nose and pointed ears told me that our patrol base wasn't far and that I could stop walking soon. I liked that green goblin guy.

I went into the course a lean and mean 205 pounds, and three months later I tipped the scale at 175 pounds. We ate two MREs (meal ready to eat) a day. I had a notebook that was for classes about patrolling, but it doubled as my letter-writing paper, which then acted as my food fantasy journal. I wrote to anyone I loved in the world about all the carbs I was going to eat. I wanted to make french fries deep fried in duck fat, and to garnish a New York-style stuffed-crust pepperoni pizza with those bad boys. I wanted a cake that had half a box of Double Stuf Oreos crushed and mixed into the batter. The Oreo frosting would have more crushed cookies mixed into the cream, and once the frosting was spread, entire Oreos would be placed on top as the pièce de résistance. If there is ever a cook or a chef in need of inspiration, they should go to a Ranger School graduation and ask about the wildest food fantasies the students had.

Eventually there weren't any sharp hunger pains, just a dull hollow feeling that never went away, and I found that my real nemesis was the

CHAPTER 5

lack of sleep. Usually, you can expect one or the other to come to the surface. Students self-identify as a hungry or sleepy Ranger, and man was I sleepy. If *hangry* is an acceptable mashup of *hungry* and *angry*, so too is being *slangry* . . . or maybe it's *angreepy*. Sleep is the key to health; it regulates hormones and balances our mood. The human body can go weeks without food, but sleep will kill you almost as fast as not drinking water.

As for the summer and winter debate, I have my answer. Cold breaks a person the way heat can't, and November and December are cold times in the mountains of Georgia. Prolonged exposure to cold brings someone to the edge of their soul. Our ancestors knew we couldn't adapt to or beat the cold, so our response to it is primal. No biological development changed our bodies to withstand it. Cold remains our nemesis. Wet and cold is the worst combination imaginable. After ten days of thirty-three-degree weather and constant rain, one morning I tried to tie my boots in my patrol base and found that my waterlogged and frozen skin cut like butter when I pulled the cords of my boot laces tight. I had to ask a friend to tie my boots for me. I wouldn't think as a grown man I would need to ask another man to tie my shoes for me, but it made sense now why my dad bought me a good pair of gloves and told me to have a good Ranger buddy.

And yet, when I was exposed to the worst of what Ranger School had to offer, I found myself doing the very thing a leader can't do when times are tough. I withdrew into myself and lived inside my head—in my own silent hell. The inner solitude that had created my inner critic and kept me from connecting with Lou and the others had kept me from being a team player here too. We depended on each other to carry extra ammunition, radio equipment, heavier machine guns, ropes, and everything else we needed on missions. Instead of being the first person to volunteer to take the heaviest item, I hung in the back, waiting to pitch in once everyone else had chosen their extra weight. I didn't have my Ranger buddy eat his meal first while I stood the first watch at our fighting position. I didn't ask guys in my squad how they were doing or if they needed anything of mine from the limited medical supplies we were allowed to have.

What sealed my fate was getting caught sleeping in security. It was after two days of no sleep. Not a wink of it, and not a drop of caffeine or nicotine to artificially stimulate my will to be alert. We'd also spent two days walking up mountains, doing ambushes, and patrolling. We were soaked through the bone and chafing everywhere. I was in security, watching my sector alone with no Ranger buddy, lying next to a tree. The sun was breaking through the clouds, and for the first time the temperature rose to about forty degrees. I was a lizard in the sun, and my cold blood ran warm as nature wrapped her blanket around me and snuggled me into the forest floor. My head bobbed, and I propped it up with one hand. Big mistake. That became my pillow. I opened my eyes, rolled to my right, and flagged down my team leader.

"I need someone to strong point with me—I'm falling asleep man," I said.

"Okay, I'll get someone."

Sleeping in security is blasphemy. It's heresy. Witchcraft. The single most sacrilegious, unforgivable sin that can be done while in a patrol base. And—like the deepest, darkest, most shame-producing events in our lives—just about every infantryman who is honest with himself has done it before.

But not all get caught.

The next time my eyes opened, it was to a Ranger Instructor with his finger on the trigger of my weapon. I had been caught red-handed and guilty as sin. By trying to pull my trigger, he demonstrated that the enemy could have snuck up on me, killed me, and then killed my friends. That's why sleeping in security is the unforgivable sin of the infantryman, the guerrilla, or the freedom fighter. Because sleeping in security kills your friends. It creates a gap in security when other people depend on you to cover your sector, and anyone who is willing to kill their friends isn't someone to keep around.

Later, when the recycles stood huddled around shivering outside

CHAPTER 5

of the headquarters building, I discovered I was the only student to have recycled for two reasons: I had failed patrols as both a weapons squad leader and as a platoon leader, but most crushing of all, I had a second reason for being recycled: my squad had voted that I was a bad teammate. These two reasons for recycling made me the single worst Ranger School candidate in my class. There isn't much use in being a leader if you are not only incompetent but also completely despised. The shame was incredible.

A reputation is a hell of a thing to repair. It takes a long time to earn a good one, and you can lose it quickly. And God help you if you are stuck trying to repair the damage of a bad one. When confronted by the reality of what my squad mates thought about me, I had two choices: I could believe them and take their harsh words to heart, find the truth in them, take ownership, and then move forward with a plan to change, or I could call them all bad names and blame them for causing me to stay in the school longer. Seeing my squad mates leave the barracks and get onto the buses that would take them to Florida (the next and final phase) while I was left in the mountains to think about my failure was a tough pill to swallow. I felt jealous and resentful.

The hardest part about failing peers is that the path toward redemption is not obvious. I failed patrolling. I knew I had to double down on my knowledge of tactics and to take more responsibility for what my squad and platoon members did while I was leading them. But peer evaluations? How could I change my character? How could I stop the flawed parts of my personality on a dime? My teammates plainly told me I had failed in their eyes, which was the truth presented in very uncomfortable terms. It was up to me to fix myself.

There was a chaplain that went through Ranger School with me. A chaplain's only job is to minister to the soldiers and to tend to their "flock" as strict noncombatants. They aren't allowed to carry weapons in the military, so he had to have an exemption to carry one in training—mostly because he didn't need to be a Ranger. He didn't need this school to make him a more qualified infantryman. He chose the suffering of Ranger School voluntarily because he believed the credibility of earning a Ranger Tab would allow him to reach tough soldiers and have tough conversations with soldiers who otherwise would not share their personal struggles with him. And he hardly ever complained about anything.

He sat next to me one night as we cleaned weapons before he moved forward to the next phase, and I stayed behind to recycle. The shame and resentment I was feeling were blinding. I knew he had rated me low on peer evaluations, but he didn't seem to hate me. He was trying to encourage me. We talked for a bit about what I could do better for my next squad and platoon.

"It'll be all right," he added. "You're putting too much pressure on yourself because of your dad."

He wasn't wrong. He knew how badly I wanted to earn my Ranger Tab—like I had to earn it, or I could never show up to Thanksgiving again. My self-talk wasn't helpful. There had only ever been one course for me—one plan, one way to do things. I had to earn my tab the way a fish has to learn to swim. Instead of recognizing what I was feeling and letting that simple recognition act like a kettle letting off steam, I wallowed. I boiled over. My inner critic started talking thirty minutes before sunrise at *stand to*, when we woke up, and only stopped during the few fitful hours of interrupted sleep I got each night.

So when the chaplain told me I was putting too much pressure on myself, I heard that I wasn't good enough. After all, we all have pressure. We all deal with stress. I still struggle with contemporary buzzwords like self-care, self-love, self-compassion, healing, trauma, and mental health. They carry a stigma that makes them seem bastardized into impotence. A melodramatic signal of moral virtue. It seemed to me that the chaplain was telling me to chill out, like somehow a divine intervention would intercede on my behalf if only I surrendered. He didn't tell me how to stop putting unnecessary pressure on myself, but to be fair, I never asked. Mentally and emotionally, I wasn't in a place to hear his truth yet.

CHAPTER 5

I had one week to recover before my next class started. I ate an MRE for Thanksgiving, and because I had been so hungry days earlier, I didn't mind celebrating turkey day by eating food out of a bag. I slept twelve hours at night and pulled off two one-hour cat naps throughout the day. When I had time that wasn't eating or sleeping, I read. I devoured four books in four days as a way to escape the mental burden of thinking about the pain that was looming.

The books were in a little box, all leftover by recycled students who'd had people mail them while they waited. I rummaged through our little library each day and couldn't believe what I found. One was written a Navy SEAL who went to Ranger School and recycled—a guy who had literally gone through what I was going through. The book was *The Trident: The Forging and Reforging of a Navy SEAL Leader* by Jason Redman, and his personal story gave me the strength I needed to take a hard look in the mirror.

Jason wanted to be a Navy SEAL his whole life. He worked hard to pass BUDs and earned a commission as an officer after spending years in the teams as an enlisted man. But despite his outward success, he had allowed his motives to be corrupted. He wanted to be a badass. He already was, but it wasn't good enough. He wanted to be combat-proven as an aggressive leader. Blinded by ego, he made a mistake on a deployment, and he was punished. His chain of command figured Ranger School was a good dumping ground for a SEAL who needed an attitude adjustment. It was one hell of a penance. He hit the same lows I was experiencing, and it was his strength to change himself that I leaned on as a frustrated recycle in the Appalachian Mountains.

Few people will experience the amount of stress and physical deprivation that happens in Ranger School. But there are plenty of other ways that pain presents. You might have a nagging sports injury or a medical condition. Maybe your home isn't a safe place. School hallways have plenty of opportunities for bullies to act badly. Pain is a soul stripper, no matter how it appears. It peels away our ego and consciousness until all that remains are the raw edges of the soul. In that moment of pain, it's hard to hear or see anything else. My soul was pretty raw. I was ashamed that my peers had rated me low. And I was afraid. All I could think about for the week I recycled was that I didn't want to go back out into the cold. Ultimately, I was frustrated that events outside my control had caused me to fail my patrols. And with that small seed of frustration, I knew I had a choice to make. Was bitterness and resentment going to win out, or was humility going to carry me through the process of redemption? Could I hear the priest's words and not put pressure on myself?

I later defined pressure as trying to control events that were outside my control. That seemed less spiritually nebulous to me. If I was chosen to lead a patrol and it was thirty-three degrees and raining and the guys hadn't slept in two days, so be it. I couldn't control the weather, but I could control the plan I made and the actions I took on the patrol. I couldn't make mountains any easier to climb, but I could stick to my mantra of *don't look up* and just focus on what was in front of me, or I could repeat another mantra and remind myself that *everything ends*. I was scared I wouldn't earn a tab, so I decided that I would have to plan my life without one. I had to see myself fail completely. I had to let go of the enormous desire to earn the credibility and validation of a tab and know that, even if I failed, I would still have worth.

As I felt myself loosen the grip of pressure, I found I could be just a bit more in the moment and lean into the suffering in a new way. I learned how to keep going when things were hard. Pain ends. Suffering ends. Everything ends. Anxiety produces the feeling that the crushing weight we are experiencing won't end. That there is no expiration date on suffering. Anxiety chokes out our mind's ability to generate hope the way a grappler can rear naked choke an opponent. Anxiety strangles you. I wanted to go home. I wanted to keep crafting a happy place in my mind, a distracting mental retreat that pulled me away from the present instead of sinking me deeper into the moment. But that simple mantra—*everything ends*—was the self-talk I had been missing.

The military camp that I was recycled at is a small place and

CHAPTER 5

didn't have much infrastructure to it other than a barracks building, a chow hall, a headquarters building, and a few smaller administrative buildings built into the slope of the hills with a helicopter pad that two UH-60 Blackhawks could fly out of. It was sparse and barren. Nothing about it connected me to the outside world. We only had letters and a payphone that we used with a prepaid phone card. No internet, no cell phones, no television. It was a world all its own, isolated and remote.

Mountains can be beautiful places. But when you have a hundred-pound backpack on, are underfed and haven't slept, and it's thirty-three degrees out and raining, mountains change. They aren't as beautiful when you are soaked to the bone. They are a soul-crushing monument to the superior strength of nature. When you are forced to climb those mountains in those conditions, you learn lessons. One is that you don't look up. You never look up.

Climbing a mountain is simple, and it's done the same way every time: put one foot in front of the other until you reach the top. That's the recipe. But you have to keep your head down as you walk. Every time I searched above me for a clearing in the tree line, I tricked myself. Every time, I picked a false summit. And when you get to what you think is the top and there is still more mountain above you, that's more soul-crushing than if your house burned down in winter. If you think too far into the future and lose sight of the progress just one second can bring, you run the risk of being crushed by the totality of the pain still in store. Ranger School taught me that all pain ends. All pain somehow leaves out the backdoor in an Irish goodbye. Endurance comes from having the right perspective.

Suffering without an end date is its own form of torture, but real hope is found in not looking for the end. Real hope is found when you put one foot in front of the other and commit to the next step, the next three feet of progress that each stride can bring. Time doesn't matter; there is no stopwatch counting the seconds until the suffering ends. You have to finish, and that's the only way through hell. You don't look around and compare how other people are doing. You don't wish for it to be over. You put your head down and do the simplest thing you can do. You take the smallest measurement of progress in stride.

On my second time through the mountain phase, I no longer looked to escape the suffering of the moment. Instead, I leaned into it. I didn't pray for the end to come, for the suffering to end. I had to identify things I could control and the things I could not, and stoicism brought me into the present moment, where I had choices I could make. I couldn't control how bad the weather would be, but I could make sure my extra socks were dry and waterproofed. I couldn't control how much food I ate or how much sleep I got. And I could control my attitude.

Calling someone a stoic can conjure an image of a person silent in the midst of suffering. A man of few words, capable of enduring pain and torment with the apparent ambivalence of a cow standing in the rain (credit to Tim Ferriss for that metaphor). Like my EMT teammate Lou, we see stoics as someone who can be thrust into terrible situations and come out like a cowboy smoking a cigarette—calm, cool, and collected. On my second time through the mountains, I learned that the inner calm at the levels attributed to a stoic doesn't come from a commitment to silence. Stoicism isn't about projecting a fake masculine endurance with few words and many grunts and thousand-yard stares off into the horizon. I learned that by focusing on the moment, shortening my time span of thought, and not letting my mind wander—past the next meal, the next map check, past the cadence of putting my right foot in front of my left foot—I could do more than I thought possible with less self-inflicted suffering.

So how does a stoic grapple with the ups and downs of human emotion? We aren't robots controlled by artificial intelligence. We are human, aware of our feelings, sentient of the power of love and loss, joy and sorrow. We feel. And because we feel, we don't live like animals, but as men and women that provide and nurture. Epictetus wrote:

Events don't disturb people; the way they think about events does. Even death is not frightening by itself. But our view of death, that

CHAPTER 5

it is something we should be afraid of frightens us. So when we are frustrated, angry, or unhappy, let's hold ourselves responsible for these emotions because they are the result of our judgments. No one else is responsible for them. When you blame others for your negative feelings, you are being ignorant. When you blame yourself for your negative feelings, you are making progress. You are being wise when you stop blaming yourself or others.

When suffering is survived properly, it actually hardens us to the circumstances that produced it. A single parent comes to a confident belief that they can work two jobs, make meals, and drive kids to soccer practice day in and day out. An entrepreneur comes to find clients and build a business from scratch, regardless of whether anyone else believed in them. An athlete learns how to play hurt, doing what it takes to keep their spot on the team. Suffering produces the grit it takes to grind it out and make it to the other side.

When suffering is survived properly, it also softens us. Once we've experienced a specific form of pain, we are able to recognize it in others. We can hear the silent screams that others are stifling because we ourselves once suffered in silence. Single parents know what sacrifices it takes to provide for and parent children on their own. Entrepreneurs recognize their own bold spirit in the start-up community around them. Athletes know the long road to recovery and the competitive drive that makes them destroy their bodies for the love of the game.

No one likes getting hurt, physically or emotionally. But life is going to throw its share of punches our way. Food and sleep deprivation, as well as exposure to the weather, are key ingredients meant to induce the maximum stress possible for Ranger students. Loneliness, anxiety, fear, grief, depression, and addiction are common ingredients we all face. Removing the emotional reaction to the pain we encounter allows us to learn lessons so we don't have to experience them at the same intensity again, and this learning makes us wise.

When Marcus Aurelius wrote, "It is not death that a man should fear, but he should fear never beginning to live," he was offering the wisdom that life is too short to be bound by fear. In order to bring moments of extreme pressure into property clarity, stoics compare their problems to the prospect of death. After all, death comes whether we are ready or not. Reflecting on death shouldn't be depressing; it acts as a nudge toward courage. The first time you ask a girl out and aren't sure she will say yes is a terrifying process. She might say no. She might like Timmy from third period who made her laugh in class. Who knows—but your mind certainly has a dozen excuses to hold you back in a state of fear. A hero will encounter the possibility of failure at every momentous decision on their journey. Any failure short of actual death is not a failure but a chance to learn, a chance to improve and become wiser.

Epictetus taught his students, "Whenever you face difficult situations in life, remember the prospect of death and other major tragedies that can and do happen to people. You will see that, compared to death, none of the things you face in life is important enough to worry about." Death is a reminder that the life we have now should not be wasted. Heroes don't wish away their present to transport themselves to their future triumphs. They are present. Soaking in the lessons that life is presenting them and becoming wiser, more courageous, more just, and more balanced each day.

The pressure of death is the due date of your homework assignment. Our life will end one day, regardless of whether we have completed our heroic journey. If you remember your death properly, you shouldn't become depressed. It creates a deeper appreciation for the life you have, the people around you, and the goals you want to achieve. When we remember that we will die. It is just a reminder that no matter how bad things are, they aren't the end. You've only got one life to live, so make it a good one. Make it a wise one. Check your fears, and when those fears don't serve a purpose for you, shed them. No matter how crushing the failure, at least you escaped with your life. So you might as well try to suffer as little as possible while you have it. And you might as well be something positive for those around you.

CHAPTER 5

That is how a stoic embraces the events that happen outside of our control with a level head and an untroubled spirit. It's not a feudal admonishment that you should not try to improve your lot if things aren't going well for you. It's not a hall pass for continuing destructive behavior that you know you shouldn't engage in. And it's certainly not a wishful way of thinking good things into coming your way. It's easy for me to nitpick at the fact I'm unhappily single and want a dating relationship, but I remind myself there are plenty of couples who wish they were single. Our happiness is not found in external circumstances—another person, more money, or a nicer car. Epictetus taught, "Do not seek for everything to happen as you wish it would, but rather wish that everything happens as it actually will."

Gratitude keeps a hero's mind from becoming swamped with negativity. Today, I am alive. I will never live the same day that I lived today. I am grateful for the life I had today because tomorrow is not guaranteed. The bills I have to pay, the hours I spend behind a desk, and the stress I feel piling up in my chest all lose their sting when I remember the finite time I have left to live.

Stoicism isn't just an internal philosophy. It extends to those around us. A stoic wants other people to be fulfilled. A stoic wants those around him or her to know what a life of peace feels like. A stoic is connected to history and committed to the future by living out a present life, concerned for others. We want to take care of the environment to ensure the future of the coming generations. We want to create new technology that will advance progress and improve the quality of life for others. We want to make the cyber world a world where innocent people can't be bullied and where bad actors on the dark web can't do unspeakable things. We want our governments to respect our human rights. Looking through stoic eyes, we realize we are connected to one another. We all want to be loved. We want our families to be safe, our governments to be just, and to find love strong enough to grow old with another person.

On your heroic path, there will be acts of compassion for you to complete, because your journey is ultimately spent in service of others. There are already good works inside of you waiting to be done. Maybe you've wanted to start a nonprofit or join nongovernment organization and travel to different parts of the world providing medicine, food, and other social services to a forgotten and unseen people. Maybe there are lines of code you need to program to create a new software, app, or product that will make our lives easier, safer, and more connected. Stoics know that their heroic journey will require them to boldly serve others in the capacity that only they are capable of. Marcus Aurelius wrote, "Revere the gods, and look after each other. Life is short—the fruit of this life is a good character and acts for the common good."

The first time in the mountains, I was focused on me and me alone. I was in survival mode. I was selfish, naive, and anxious. The second time in the mountains, I had to decide from the beginning that I was strong enough to handle what was coming my way. And by doing so, I was able to put others ahead of me. Each time I did that, it was like I was proving to myself that I was bigger than I was. I was being selfish by helping others because it was helping me more than I was ever able to give them. I had to keep going no matter what by not looking up or around, but down. Focused on one foot in front of the other.

By the end, I was ranked number one in my squad for peers, passed the remainder of my patrols on my first look, and was nominated to compete for officer honor grade of my Ranger Class when I graduated. In army language, I had done well.

Our past can be a tremendous resource to change our behavior in the present moment, and that change can be the key to a better future. It might feel idealistic to think that the world can be a better place, but think about it: what would your high school look like if people gossiped less? And what if tomorrow when you show up to first period you gave someone a compliment? It's not the world around you that you are trying to change or believe could be better; it's the world you are living in now. *You* can live in a world where *you* are better, where *you* are the change you think will help others.

CHAPTER 5

Epictetus knew that his students would quit on their dreams at the onset of adversity if they didn't prepare to meet resistance to their plans. He said, "When you are about to undertake a project, consider not only what is involved now but what it would involve later. Otherwise, you will plunge in enthusiastically at the beginning and end up quitting in disgrace when things get difficult later." When we anticipate hardships and failure, we are better able to complete our heroic journey of a thousand miles, knowing that life could easily make the journey that much longer.

Seneca knew life could always be worse, "Rehearse them in your mind: exile, torture, war, shipwreck. All the terms of our human lot should be before our eyes." How much money do you have saved in case you get fired from your job? How much food do you have in storage in case a natural disaster shuts off your power? The stress you are capable of handling as a young person is preparing you for the gauntlets you will experience later in life. You are hardening in the places you need to harden so that you aren't naive as your world intensifies. You are learning to identify where compassion can guide you to make better decisions, to be a better leader, and to create a home that's worth coming home to each evening.

You will have consequences for bad decisions, but the worst monster you will contend with on your journey is your inner critic. Will you hate yourself for what you've done, or can you find a way to show yourself compassion? Shame drags us into the depth of depression, and when we are depressed, we are capable of anything. But self-compassion starts with forgiveness. Ask God, your neighbor, your family, your lover, your ex, your coworkers to forgive your mistakes. Then turn to the work of forgiving yourself.

You have a strength within you that can endure more than you know. You will find who you really are when the chips are down. When everything is stripped away from you, you'll find that you still have a strength within you that can't be taken away. You will encounter stress and anxiety as you plan out your life and have to take steps into adulthood. Keep going. Take courage in the fact that when you are at your lowest and it feels like you are climbing a mountain, all you have to do is put one foot in front of the other. Your suffering will end. One day you will wake up and it will be the last day your heart will ache from your breakup. One day you will wake up and hear birds chirp in the morning, and you will realize that winter is gone and that spring has come without any warning other than the small song of a creature that flies with the seasons. The beauty of shortening your time horizon is that you gain altitude over the mountains of your problems at the smallest increment possible. One day you will wake up and the cumulated progress you've willed yourself into achieving will bring the summit into view.

CHAPTER 6

THE PRIVILEGE OF A LIFETIME IS BEING WHO YOU ARE.

—JOSEPH CAMPBELL

On September 10, 2001, my dad was assigned to report to the Pentagon from his home in Kansas. My parents were separated, on their way to getting a divorce, and my brother and I lived with my mom in a suburb of southwest Baltimore. Like most separated couples, they communicated poorly with each other. I had intermittent contact with him, but knew I'd be able to see him after he arrived on the tenth.

On September 11, 2001, I was in second grade. I remember finishing up my breakfast and getting ready to start my first homeschool lesson for the day when news of the terrorist attack was broadcast live to a grieving nation. Our TV was old—a big box that had bunny-ear antennae that required skillful manipulation to get the standard TV channels. As the screen flickered and waved, I barely grasped what I was seeing.

My mother began frantically calling my father's cell phone. He didn't pick up. Then a distraught call from my aunt brought news that my uncle wasn't picking up his phone either. He was in the Marine Corps and although he wasn't stationed at the Pentagon, sometimes he went there for work.

For hours, I waited and watched. Like every kid in school that day, I was confused and trying to understand the destruction I was witnessing. Like thousands of us, I was also trying to comprehend the death it could bring to my family. It was personal.

Eventually, the phone rang. My aunt was on the line.

"He's fine! Frank is fine!" my aunt said.

Later, the phone rang again. I could tell my mom didn't want to answer it. Slowly, she picked up the receiver and took the call.

It was my dad. He was okay. They talked for a moment, and then he talked with me and my older brother.

"Where are you?" I asked.

"I'm in DC."

"You weren't at the Pentagon?"

"No, I had a flat tire driving to DC. I missed my report day yesterday. I wasn't there this morning."

We hung up, and for the rest of the day we watched the news as America came to grips with the reality of what had happened. Why had people attacked my family? Who were they? Why did they kill so many innocent people?

That was the day I knew what I would become. I would be a soldier like my father. A fighter like the men who deployed weeks after the attack to bring retribution to the Taliban government and Al Qaida terrorist network. I was obsessed. One day, I would be a warrior.

I didn't know what it really meant to be a soldier. I didn't know what deployments would be like, the training it would take, and the cost it would levy on my personal life. I just knew I wanted to become a soldier, and that's it. To me, becoming a warrior meant I could be like the men in my family, my role models. It meant I would be tough and brave. It meant I would learn how to fight and to be a leader. There was no blood lust motivation to go to war. I simply never wanted to feel like my family was unsafe again. I also realized there are people who want to harm innocent people and that the institutions designed

CHAPTER 6

to safeguard freedom needed people to join them. So I would.

Setting the proper expectations for your life is difficult. You don't want to set the bar so low that you never achieve your potential, but at the same time a healthy perspective is in order. What do you expect your military service will be like? Why do you want to become a cop? Do you think your start-up will take off like Facebook did? Do you think your first painting will be the Mona Lisa? Do you think that being a lawyer is about flashy cars and nice suits? In Steven Pressfield's book *Turning Pro*, he makes the distinction between an amateur and a professional. An amateur wants recognition and rewards for their work. A professional is satisfied by the work he or she does because that work is so closely aligned to their purpose that they would do it in obscurity and for free.

On your heroic journey, you will go without comfort. If you join the military, there will be times you will go without sleep, food, or shelter. Cops show up on the night shift with nothing but a coffee and dip for dinner. Doctors and nurses work incredible hours for the benefit of their patients, making their own needs secondary to those they are charged to help. Entrepreneurs sacrifice security and a comfortable life for the chance to turn an idea into a business. Artists attack each painting, each book, and each performance with the nagging thought that their next month's rent is due and they don't have the money yet.

The harder the challenge we face, the more we grow. The harder the classes we take, the more we have to study and the more we learn. The harder we work out the more our muscles grow and the better shape we get in. The more we say no to distractions and things we know we ought not to do, the more we become committed to our future.

As a slave, the hopes and dreams of freedom that Epictetus cultivated every day were courageous acts of resistance. Once he earned his freedom, he taught that "difficulty shows what men are." What type of man are you? Are you the type of person other people want around in hard times? Are you the type of woman people look to when a tough call needs to be made? Are you training to be a hero capable of completing your journey?

If you give up on your heroic calling, you are not only giving up the dream and yourself—you're refusing to fulfill your sacred vow to fight an external force. There are doubts inside of you that need to be defeated; there are mental thought patterns that are the bonds that keep you from freedom. If you don't combat self-doubt, you are losing the momentum of your heroic journey. You'll become depressed and bitter and resentful at the world around you. Instead of taking your place as a hero, you will stay small and angry at those around you who *are* trying to walk their own sacred journey. You are giving up on the sacred process of growth, and it will haunt you.

Are you leaning into your suffering or are you hiding from pain and stunting your heroic growth? When we are faced with challenges we aren't sure we can overcome, we grow. We learn, we change how we think, we get new friends and drop old friends, we move cities and leave our families behind. In short, we are willing to change ourselves to become something more than what we previously were. Our actions reveal who we are to ourselves. Heroes grow in ability through the challenges they overcome. That is the source of their confidence and their power.

Difficult circumstances reveal a person's real character. When things go wrong, when businesses stop making money, when love leaves a relationship, we have the responsibility to choose how we will react. As stoicism teaches, we don't control things that happen *to* us, only the reaction we have *within* us. Dr. Jordan B. Peterson is a Canadian psychologist and bestselling author of *Maps of Meaning* and *12 Rules for Life.* His message resonates with his audience because he encourages young people to adopt a level of responsibility sufficient to give their lives meaning. He teaches that responsibility creates a sense of purpose that makes the suffering of life worth the price. "Adopt responsibility for your own well-being, try to put your family together, try to serve your community, try to seek eternal truth . . . .. That's the sort of thing that can ground you in your life, enough so that you can withstand the difficulty of life."

When I recycled in Ranger School, I could have blamed my squad mates. But the more blame I put on others, the heavier I felt. The moment I took responsibility for my shortcomings, the better I felt. I actually gained confidence by acknowledging that I didn't know everything. I began to grow. I began to view the people around me as people worth taking care of, rather than people who stood in my way. Accepting your role on your journey is admitting that your journey isn't just about you. It's about those you can help. Life is best lived in a symbiotic relationship.

Jim Rohn was a motivational speaker in the 1970s who focused on personal growth. He said that we are the average of the five people we associate with most. Your friend group in high school, work, or college can get you into a lot of trouble. Or they can be the group of people who encourage you to work out harder and perform better and will hold you accountable. Your friends can be tremendous allies on your journey. When you are suffering and it feels like your soul is being stripped bare, your friends can be there to remind you of who you are. They can ground you and encourage you to keep moving forward. Friends who see you for who you really are, are more valuable than a bigger salary or winning the lottery. Good friends can save you. But not everyone in life will be a friend, and not everyone you call a friend will be a good one.

When people blame their failures on others, do you let their attitude rub off on you or do you take responsibility for the things you can change and build the discipline to do so? You can choose to have a victim mentality and blame other people for your debt, for your hardships, for your suffering and live a life starting at an early age that won't amount to much utility for anyone else. Or you can stoically take responsibility for your life, so that one day you will be capable of taking care of yourself. If you become responsible for the safety of those around you, the care of those under your command, and the success of the mission, that mindset is not a switch you can flip on when you need it. It takes time to build it, starting at a young age. The old adage that idle hands are the devil's playthings should keep you stoically tinkering away on your soul and diligently focused on the work ahead of you.

Responsibility is not easy or enjoyable. Even something as simple as chores can become a challenge. Taking the trash out of the house, placing it into the garbage can outside, and then taking it down to the curb isn't fun. Epictetus taught us, "Don't explain your philosophy. Embody it." That's what we are doing when we commit to the little things. We are embodying our personal discipline because how we do *anything* is how we do *everything*.

Courage is the most obvious virtue that is applicable to your heroic journey and needs the least explanation. We know soldiers, marines, airmen, and sailors need to be brave in war. Cops have to run toward the sound of gunfire, not away from it. Firefighters run into burning buildings. Artists and entrepreneurs live courageously in uncertainty. Your heroic journey will demand you demonstrate courage, no matter your path. And courage might not always take the first form that comes to mind. Courage starts on the inside and works its way into our actions. Starting a family takes courage. Changing careers takes courage. Going to a school away from your family, standing up to an injustice, or spending your time differently than your peers do can all be courageous. Stepping out of the world of the comfortable and familiar and into someplace new takes bravery. And for young people, just learning to trust yourself that you are in fact hearing the calling of your heroic journey takes an element of courage.

There's a contest between achievement and fulfillment that requires even more courage on our path. Achievement makes us worry about the outcome. The idea that we need to accomplish our goals in order to be happy is only a half-truth. There's more to life than getting what we want—if you cross enough goals off your checklist, you'll find that they actually lose their luster. That isn't to say you won't achieve. You've got a hunger inside of you to make the most of your life; go for it! You're meant to dream big—without limits. This eagerness to rush into their potential is common for young people on the first few steps of their heroic journey. But you can't get stuck on the end before you've set out in the beginning. Often if we analyze our desires, we find out we want what we don't have simply *because* we don't have it. We think that if we get more money, more friends, more clothes, we will feel better by gaining the self-respect we hope those items will offer us.

The antidote to a wasted life is to stoically attack each day containing the fury of a lifetime within a twenty-four-hour period of time. Seneca wrote, "Begin at once to live, and count each separate day as a separate life." It's not that we need to go skydiving every day, spend our last dollar to buy lottery tickets, or quit school to make the most out of life right now by doing extreme things. Stoicism doesn't call us to be reckless and impulsive but to enjoy our youth without the fear of missing out.

When we put in the hours of work, doing the thankless tasks that need to be done without seeking recognition, we are building the moral courage to become more resilient. If you want to become a writer, write every day. If you want to become a professional athlete, practice every day. If you want to become a self-sustaining homesteader, plant your first seeds. Epictetus could have wasted a lot of time wishing for freedom as a slave instead of living free within his own mind. But he knew a lifetime committed to excellence isn't easy. He said, "You would like to win at the Olympics? So would I. Who wouldn't? But consider what you need to do now and what you need to do later on before committing to it. You have to submit yourself to rigorous discipline, maintain a strict diet, avoid rich but tasty food, exercise long hours in inclement weather, refrain from drinking alcohol, and give up some of your social life. In short, you should hand yourself over to your trainer." If you believe your destiny is to be a warrior, entrepreneur, artist, mother, father, lover, healer, athlete, or protector, you will have a lot of hard work ahead of you.

You will have to grind through pain and loneliness and failure—sometimes all three will crash down on you at once. But you are stronger than you think. You are braver than you know.

You know you are connected to your purpose when you fall asleep at the end of a day and have the strength to wake up the next morning and do it all over again. The quiet desperation that you feel sitting in traffic, driving to work to a job that is unfulfilling, surrounded by people who aren't like you and who won't understand you—that's you living a life out of alignment for your life's calling. We all have chores and commutes and responsibilities that cause resentment. That's not the point. If you can't find meaning and purpose in the little things you do in life, and if the mundane is exacting a cost on your mental and physical health, that's a hint your life isn't what it should be. Is your soul being crushed? Is the fantasy of the life you could live more powerful than the actual life you are currently living?

With that said, a hint that you are on the right track is when you do things that feel as if time doesn't matter. It's obliterated by any conscious metric, the way two lovers sitting across each other at a restaurant peel their gaze away from each other for the first time and realize they are the last customers in the restaurant and the wait staff is closing down for the night. I fell into my journey as a warrior like it was love at first sight. The desire to join the military, and even certain units, compelled me the way seeing someone walk into the room for the first time can make us tumble head over heels in love. The romance of life's journey showed itself to me, and I never looked back. I never understood why in sixth grade my classmates didn't know what they wanted to be when they grew up. I'm grateful I was found by my purpose at a young age because I didn't waste time figuring things out. I was a faithful lover committed to the relationship of the journey. There was no other path for me.

Love binds you to tasks that are difficult and unpleasant. Loving what you do is why writers write words that no one may ever read. It's why painters paint canvases that will stay in their studios. It's why chefs start at the bottom of the hierarchy of their thankless profession. It's why doctors go through a decade of expensive schooling before ever

CHAPTER 6

getting to practice. It's why athletes train their bodies and risk injury in competition. Finding your purpose and committing to it carries the same significance as finding your soulmate. You commit yourself. You promise to be faithful in the good times and the bad. You promise before the god you believe in and the family that supports you that you will do the impossible and take two lives and make it into one. That's what you do when you find your purpose. You commit to the path of your life over other potential paths that may exist. You acknowledge the trials that will come because you have chosen the heroic journey, and you know the sacrifices that will be demanded from you. But when you commit to that level, you also know you won't be alone. You won't have to struggle along on your journey. You will have a god that backs you. Mentors will teach you and open doors for you. Friends will celebrate with you when good things happen and be there when bad things come.

Like love, the harder you look and the more you demand your purpose to show up, the harder it will be to find and keep it. Your purpose will find you. Your purpose will snatch you up. It will see you first and it will love you first. It will see the work ahead of you and will love you nonetheless. It won't let you go. It will guide you into the future, as committed to you as you are to it.

Not everyone's purpose finds them at seven or eight years old—but being that young doesn't invalidate the calling. Hannibal Barca was an ancient Carthaginian general whose legendary ability to defeat larger and better-supplied armies almost eradicated the Roman Republic. And he made his vow—to make the enemies of his people his enemies and to fight against the same men as his father—at an alarmingly young age. As the legend goes, one day his father—Hamilcar Barca—brought young Hannibal in front of a sacred altar. As the hot North African sun shined down, the young boy made a solemn vow. With all the fervor and honest commitment an eight-year-old could muster, he promised to live his life locked in the mortal struggle of fighting for freedom against the expansionist Roman Republic. Hannibal assumed a generational burden of fighting in conflicts the older generation didn't finish and committed to the warrior's path before he was even old enough to join the army.

Hannibal would go on to become one of the ancient world's most renowned generals. At the battle of Cannae, he used a double envelopment maneuver on the Roman legions and massacred his encircled enemies. So terrifying was the slaughter and so horrible was their imminent death that legend says Roman legionaries stooped down in formation, dug a hole in the sand, and buried their own heads in sand so that they could commit suicide by suffocation rather than be butchered by Hannibal's soldiers. Hannibal led a campaign of terror that would keep the Roman people locked in a state of panic and fear for twenty years. The tactics he used to fight against the Romans are still studied by modern military leaders. But Hannibal paid a heavy price for his fame and success. He witnessed the complete and utter destruction of his nation. He fled his homeland and lived out his last few years a wanted and hunted man. Eventually, he took his own life in a house surrounded by Roman soldiers rather than give them the satisfaction of capturing him alive.

Hannibal answered the calling of his life. He could have had a different life. He could have bought a vineyard and spent his life cultivating the earth in peace and comfort with a family. But the power of choosing a purpose in his youth was that he did not waste any time. He was able to leverage the bulk of his life committed to becoming the best fighter, general, and leader he could be. War demanded excellence from him, so he became excellent.

While youth is a gift, it's worth investigating whatever you feel is pulling you into your future when you are young. Because not all forces are created equal. Pride, greed, fame, and self-aggrandizement can be powerful motivators, but those types of motivations crumble on first contact with the enemy. Something deeper is required to pull you years into your future—something not centered on achievement and status. You don't need fame. You don't need recognition or likes or

CHAPTER 6

attaboys. Your transformation happens when you realize the path ahead of you will not be lined with adoring fans or cheering spectators. The journey can be lonely and confusing. But despite all of that, you know that you have within you the acorn that can sprout into a mighty—heroic—oak.

The trick is to allow that growth to unfold over time. Many philosophers over the centuries have reflected on the feeling of yearning for the future. Seneca wrote this about sacrificing enjoying the present moment: "True happiness is to enjoy the present, without anxious dependence upon the future, not to amuse ourselves with either hopes or fears, but to rest satisfied with what we have, which is sufficient, for he that is so wants nothing. The greatest blessings of mankind are within us and within our reach. A wise man is content with his lot, whatever it may be, without wishing for what he has not."

When we are young, we are great at spotting problems. Politics, the environment, and social injustices ignite our passion. We are full of piss and vinegar, ready to charge head-first into the breach. We don't think strategically; we think tactically—find the problem, fix the problem. But problems are complex and layered, like onions and ogres. Life can be very bad. Places like Venezuela, Syria, and Ukraine do not provide cushy suburban childhoods or the idealistic romantic rural upbringing. There are places where rockets blow up schools and neighborhoods run out of food. Children in certain areas of the world experience extreme suffering at the hands of cruel governments and genocidal violent extremist organizations. Children in our own country experience lives riddled with gang violence, absent fathers, drug use, and the effects of cyclical poverty. A hero looks at the suffering around them and sets out on their heroic journey to heal, help, and uplift others. In the process, the hero faces their own adversity that builds them into someone who is capable of solving complex problems and leading others on the path to progress.

If it bothers you to see helpless people pushed around by bullies, if genocide is more than a news headline to you, if you recognize the absolute disaster authoritarian regimes pose to the world, then you have the opportunity to build yourself into someone capable of resisting them. Those are problems that you can help solve one day. That level of meaning will literally infuse you with purpose from the moment you wake up, through the workouts you complete, and to the last moment before you go to bed. If you commit to becoming wise, your youth isn't wasted at all. That means acquiring a certain form of patience that doesn't view *any* change as good but the *right* change as good.

The gift of youth is that you have time to prepare for the future of your choosing. Who you become is entirely up to you. Time is the one resource that can never be bought back, created, or recycled. It comes and it goes. If you wish it away, you lose it forever. But if you spend it diligently preparing for your future while simultaneously living life in the joy of the moment, you'll find a tremendous balance of it in your youth. You control the opportunities you pursue, and you control the level of responsibility you accept in your life. Seneca wrote, "The whole future lies in uncertainty: live immediately." Take care of the things around you that you ought to, don't shirk responsibility, and when tasks are difficult, don't wish that they weren't. You will grow proportionally to the challenges you face.

How do you define a life well-lived? Is it measured in years or is it measured in terms less quantifiable than age? No one has the luxury of assuming that he or she will live into old age. Our best-laid plans can be cut short by events outside our control. A drunk driver at an intersection, an unforeseen war, a medical diagnosis that comes out of nowhere. Not all warriors will die in their beds of old age. Not all children will outlive their mothers. We have a role to play in this life we are given, and we don't know how long we will be on life's stage.

According to Seneca, "Life is like a play: it's not the length, but the excellence of the acting that matters." Marcus Aurelius wrote, "You could leave life right now. Let that determine what you do and say and think." Stoicism emphasizes the importance of pursuing excellence in all we do because life is a precious thing. Each moment we have with

CHAPTER 6

our family is a gift. Each moment of peace, each act of freedom we take is a reminder of the beauty in this world. Find your purpose and follow it relentlessly as soon as your North Star appears. You will be guided, you will be helped, and you will be inspired to overcome adversity and tragedy if your eyes remain fixed on the prize—if you remain focused on becoming the best version of yourself.

CHAPTER 7

DON'T BE ASHAMED TO NEED HELP. LIKE A SOLDIER STORMING A WALL, YOU HAVE A MISSION TO ACCOMPLISH. AND IF YOU'VE BEEN WOUNDED AND YOU NEED A COMRADE TO PULL YOU UP? SO WHAT?

—MARCUS AURELIUS

Ernest Hemingway served in the Red Cross on the Italian front during World War I, where he was severely wounded in the leg by an artillery shell. He had seen war up close and understood it well enough to write several books about it. *For Whom the Bell Tolls* was former Senator John McCain's favorite novel. Set in the Spanish Civil War, it detailed a character who was an expert in guerrilla warfare and planned operations with native fighters against better-supplied and better-equipped enemies. And he wrote these words in *A Farewell to Arms*: "The world breaks everyone, and afterward many are strong at the broken places. But those that it will not break, it kills. It kills the very good and the very gentle and the very brave, impartially. If you are none of these, you can be sure it will kill you too, but there will be no special hurry."

Ernest Hemingway killed himself on July 2, 1961.

Here was a man who had spent his youth trying to save men in war but didn't know how to save himself from life. Hemingway had

CHAPTER 7

fame, he had money, he could travel the world, and he was the epitome of masculinity in his time. Yet beneath all outward metrics of success, none of his achievements could give him the peace he needed to continue living. How many unwritten books went to the grave with him?

My first encounter with suicide happened as an EMT when I was seventeen. The weird part about a suicide is interacting with the family of the victim. What does one say to a parent who has lost their child? What do you say to a spouse who is looking at their partner and wondering *why*? No training prepared me for those conversations.

The call came in like every other call. It was a Saturday night in the summer between my junior and senior year of high school. I was in waiting mode: sitting on the couch, watching TV, drinking a Cherry Coke, nursing a sneaking suspicion that perhaps that night might be when "the big one" would happen. That night, it was a White male, unresponsive, on the far end of town. Our crew ran to the ambulance. Lou and Jon hopped in the front, and I jumped into the back like a well-rehearsed piece of choreography.

As soon as we arrived on scene, I could smell the pungent scent of marijuana. As I rolled the stretcher to the house, a couple in their fifties were standing casually in the living room, pointing toward a bedroom door. I noticed they were completely composed, directing us toward who I assumed was their son as calmly as a road worker directs traffic around a construction site. In the bedroom, we found an overweight young man in his early twenties. Next to his bed was an Xbox, hooked up to a TV, with *Call of Duty* playing on the screen. His character was spawning and being killed over and over again as he was dying in real life on his bed.

We started giving him oxygen and positioning him to be moved onto the stretcher, while being careful not to get stuck by a dirty needle hiding somewhere in the folds of the bedsheets and blanket. When we got him onto the stretcher, John started to take him outside into the ambulance, where the supervisor was prepared to treat him.

"Stay here and find the needle" he said.

With his video game character still dying every couple of seconds in the background, I started shaking out his bed sheets and blanket. Instead of a needle, a red 12-gauge shotgun shell unceremoniously dropped onto the floor. It was ready to use, unfired, powder and shot intact. A quick glance around the room revealed what we had all missed in plain sight. A shotgun was propped next to his closet door, little more than an arm's reach from his bed. When I told my supervisor about the shotgun and shotgun shell in the bed, the conclusion he shared was that the kid was prepared to finish the job with the gun if the drugs didn't do the trick. A suicide isn't always obvious. Not every person that commits suicide will leave behind a note that explains why they did what they did to those they leave behind. I never found a note in his room. Eventually I found the needle stuck to his pillow. I put it in a sharps container so that it wouldn't stick me and transfer any diseases it might carry.

"What's going on?" the mother asked as I came out of the room and walked toward the front door. She had a California surfer dude slur to her words. She could barely stand upright.

I was blown away. No awkward, painful question from a family member had ever come close to that one. She was so high that she couldn't comprehend that her son had just killed himself in her house. She was oblivious to the tragedy of it all.

"What do you mean?" I asked, my fist clenched at my side.

"What are the cops doing outside my house?" she asked.

"Ask them," I said bluntly. "I'm an EMT, and I'm here because your son killed himself." I hoped my words would have some sort of shocking effect, but they didn't.

The dad was only slightly more sober than the mother. He was probably the one who had called 911. He was equally a piece of shit.

"Don't let the cops come in here, man," he said as I shut the door behind me.

Sometimes it's the things left unsaid that speak the loudest. Neither of the parents asked about their son. Neither of them asked

CHAPTER 7

which hospital we were going to. There was no emotion on either of their faces. They weren't in shock. They weren't upset. They were just checked out. Indifferent. And indifference is the antithesis to real love.

I walked outside and handed Jon the plastic box containing the dirty needle. I told the cops about the shotgun and shell and about the parents not wanting police inside the house.

Inside the ambulance, the supervisor administered Narcan. The young man's body convulsed as his muscles spasmed. It was like his internal engine had stalled out at a red light. He never woke up.

Suicide is a lonely act, even when we aren't alone. The patient had parents, and he had friends online that he could play video games with. But despite others being around, they weren't actually plugged in. I can't say what he felt with any certainty, but my assessment is that he felt unloved by his parents and lacked real connection with friends in the actual world and not in the virtual reality of video games. He was starving on the inside and desperately did the one thing he hoped would bring relief.

I didn't know this patient, but I still felt compassion for him. When suicide took the life of my friends, the sting was even worse.

I lost two rugby teammates to suicide. They were good dudes who shouldn't have died in the prime of their lives, yet they were the classic victims of suicide. Young men who were the least expected to struggle with demons, the epitome of strength. They were funny, outgoing, the life of the party, and the toughest sons of bitches on the rugby pitch.

The first teammate who left life too early was a jolly fellow. He was as big as the Army would allow him to be, and we needed his size as a prop—equivalent to a football lineman. Other people might have mistaken his mass as fat, but anyone who had to tackle his enormous frame knew better. He was the biggest guy completing our mandatory two-mile runs, but he was never the last one to finish. He had heart. He had completed basic training before he came to our school, enlisting in the National Guard at a young age to help pay for college, and had a plan for his life that he followed well.

When his father got laid off, he had to leave our school and go to a different college. Our team could have used his friendship and bruising tackles against our opponents, and we missed him. When word came that he had committed suicide, it was hard to process. I had heard him laugh so many times, a deep belly laugh that spread around the locker room until everyone forgot why we were laughing in the first place because our laughter was fueled by his. Where was that darkness hiding in those moments? How could it be strong enough to lurk within someone so capable of making others so happy? He looked like a young man on the right path. He looked like he had his life together. Lots of people liked him. He was a popular guy. But somewhere inside, he must have struggled to see the value within him that we all knew was there.

The second teammate was older than me. He graduated and served in the National Guard with an exceptional record. His nickname was "Wildcard" because his antics were never predictable. They weren't dangerous or indicative of being unstable; he was just an eclectic guy who always surprised people with whatever shenanigans he could cook up. He was as wild at heart as most young guys are, but he didn't try to cover it up to be cool like the rest of us did. He lived adventurously and stayed wild while we allowed ourselves to be tamed. He went on international hiking trips and served on a deployment as a sniper. When I heard of his untimely death, I thought back to a message he had sent me a few months before.

We were both in the Army, and he was at my base for a little while and wanted to meet up. But life was busy. I had to train for a selection and simultaneously prepare for a month-long training exercise in another state, so I didn't get around to seeing him. Perhaps it's easy to believe that if I had agreed to meet with him things could have turned out differently. Maybe I was the one person who could have seen through Wildcard's facade and uncovered what was really going on. Even now, if I let myself think about it I feel incredibly guilty for my choice to pass up a chance to hang out with an old friend. He had

CHAPTER 7

been in my corner, and I should have been in his.

On the rugby pitch, we had all won and lost together, but these friends lost a fight without the help of their teammates. When someone commits suicide, they leave behind all those who loved them and cared for them. The legacy of who they could have been was lost, and all that remains is the memories we hold of them. It's tempting to think that no one cares. No one loves us, no one understands, no one could possibly know the pain we are going through.

Men tend to experience depression silently, thinking that any acknowledgment of it is weakness in its most pathetic form. After all, it's just feelings, and men are in control of their feelings, right? As men we need others to respect our strength. We want our wives to think we are the baddest dude in the bar, and we want our sons to volunteer us to beat up other dads of their kindergarten classmates. As men we want to beat back darkness. But if we stare into the darkness too long, it stares back.

We all need help at times in our lives. Mental hygiene is no different from the care we take to brush our teeth and clean our bodies. It's hygiene—what we do to prevent disease and illness. At various times in history, hygiene levels have been lower than modern standards, and diseases rose as a result. So too with our mental health. When fighting for your life, you have allies. After his battle with Goliath, David wrote the promise that when we walk through the valley of the shadow of death, we shouldn't be afraid because we aren't alone. Mental health struggles can feel like a giant is standing across from us demanding combat.

The truth is: rock bottom feels different for all of us. Everyone struggles differently with their mental health, and we all manifest our pain in unique ways. It's hard to tell when rock bottom is coming for you. Mine came a few years after college, in a lonely hotel room where I was temporarily living to complete some military training. I wasn't suicidal, but I wasn't okay either. Rock bottom felt for me like I was tired, devoid of any sense of peace. Day after day, week after week, I kept the lights off in the hotel room and drank six-pack after six-pack of lukewarm beer with boxes of cold pizza left on the floor.

In an attempt to build a future where I could escape the rat race, I decided to enroll in graduate school and use the full scholarship I'd earned. Instead of finding freedom, graduate school added more crushing pressure to my already floundering life. I had finally put the last nail in the coffin of my on-again, off-again relationship with a raven-haired girl I had met in Europe. I was overworked, and because I was eating like crap and drinking so much, I gained thirty pounds in three months.

Nothing about how I felt made sense to me. I was in the Army. I was in the Infantry. I was Airborne and Ranger qualified, about to go on my first deployment overseas. For all intents and purposes, I should have been completely satisfied with my life. By all external metrics and according to everyone else, I was on my hero's path. I had accomplished every professional goal I set out for. But as I lay on my hotel bed with the TV turned on so the sound would make me feel less alone, I realized my life was out of control. I was depressed. I was anxious. I was not in a position of strength. Things had to change, I had to be the one to change them, and I didn't have a lot of time.

I had seen the consequences of losing control of mental health. I thought back to the call when I saw the soldier dying on his living room floor in front of his mother and sister. I thought about the son who had killed himself in his bed while playing *Call of Duty*. In that hotel room, I knew I didn't want to die, and I wasn't going to kill myself. But I needed the pain to stop. So I reached out for help.

Stoics are notorious for choosing hardships—such as fasting, cold baths, simple clothing, and plain food. But the stoic principle of temperance isn't a moral opposition to alcohol, drugs, sex, or anything pleasant in life. You can listen to loud music and get tattoos if you want to. In stoic terms, temperance is the removal of excess and the ability to avoid dependence on *external* things for *internal* peace. Do we drink responsibly and know when enough is enough, or do we drink to oblivion because it's the only form of stress relief strong enough to dull us for just a few hours? Do we work out to stay healthy or because body dysmorphia makes us think that we have to change ourselves into something loveable?

When I remember the monk I met in France, I think about how he lived life on his terms. He had the authority and rules and regulations of his church to abide by. He had his god that he submitted to. Yes, many of those things denied the individuality of his self-expression, but values in excess corrupt the nature of their virtue. Temperance is the ability to spot excess in all its forms, to see the exact line where power must be limited, where compassion has to turn to accountability, where self-criticism turns into self-loathing. Temperance is about moderation, learning to rely less on things and people and more on the strength of your character to find fulfillment. It builds discipline by self-denial. It is the mindful choice to leave the insatiable desire for more on the table. It means we see just how much rugged individualism, manliness, and self-reliance we should have to be successful without letting those virtues become corrupted into self-destructive behaviors.

We learn how to regulate ourselves by our culture and society. If we are lucky, we have role models in our families who have set a good example for how to do that. Mental health conversations are usually hard to have with people around us. It's taboo. We worry they will think we are weak; the stigma it all leaves is best avoided. Unfortunately, mental health is an internal battle. It's what happens when no one else is around, when the cameras are off and no social media posts are made. We can't see someone else's struggle in order to know who to pattern after. To be honest, we don't always see ourselves struggling either.

I view mental health like baking chocolate chip cookies. Different amounts of ingredients, different baking times, and even different levels of humidity can create cookies with different textures and different flavors. When you wake up and it's raining with a chill in the air that makes you want to grab a blanket and a cup of coffee, you can choose to be grateful for the day just as it is. To realize there will be rainy days and sunny days and that you can find joy in each of them. Or you can listen to the voice in your head screaming about how the day is ruined, the sun will never shine again, nothing ever goes right, and the storm will never leave. Temperance sees the part of us that is in despair and offers a way out—a way to see that it's all the same cookie, just different ingredients.

Few things are as good as we think, and few are as bad as we think. There is so much beauty around us all the time, but our thoughts drive the engine of our emotions. We feel because we think, and we think because we have trained ourselves how to think. Temperance is a way to dull the worst of those emotions and it can pull forward the best of them. We experience more when we stop demanding that all things should be perfect and pleasant.

At my lowest, I knew that several pillars in my life were eroding. Work was crushing me, my relationship was unfulfilling, and I was treating food and alcohol as emotional scapegoats. I was creating a recipe that would only lead to disaster—and soon, if I wasn't careful. My journey down that path had already started in high school. Without telling anyone about it, I'd have flashbacks to accidents and scenes from my EMT work in the middle of class. Some of them were vivid enough that I had to leave the classroom for a fake bathroom break so that other people wouldn't see my panic attacks.

I don't know your life and what you've experienced before reading this book or what you're experiencing now. I want you to know that if you've thought about harming yourself—or others for that matter—that you can and need to stop. Get help. Call, text, or email a hotline. It's urgent. The thoughts you have will soon turn to actions, if they haven't already, and that won't be good for you or anyone else. More importantly, what you are feeling won't last forever. Your present is not your future. You can heal. You can change your stars and have a future. There is value within you, and you can learn to see it and learn to offer it to the people around you who love you and need you.

CHAPTER 7

The process of repair might be the bravest thing you'll ever do in your life. The journey of healing might be the hardest thing you ever do. But a stoic isn't measured by the number of times they don't break when life is unfair. A stoic is most stoic when life breaks us and we don't quit.

The child's story of *Humpty Dumpty* comes to mind. After the great fall, "all the king's horses and all the king's men couldn't put Humpy together again." The problem I have with the story is that someone should have told our egg friend that he should never have climbed that wall in the first place. He should have been reminded that he was an egg and that eggshells break easily if they fall from great heights. Before you embark on your heroic journey, count yourself warned: if you never develop an exterior harder than an eggshell, you are going to experience catastrophe. Start while you are young enough to build more than a thin facade to protect yourself from the harsh world.

If you've lost someone you love, if you've been touched by the suffering of this world, if you already feel shattered—there is still hope. Time heals all wounds, even when the king's horses and men cannot. Seneca wrote, "Only time can heal what reason cannot." It's a fight to gain back the peace that life takes from you, and it's a fight I know your heroic spirit can win. You will one day breathe again.

The path to healing isn't always easily spotted. Pain pulls you into your inner world and the darkness of the moment. It's a helpless feeling to seem trapped in a world where nothing can be changed, least of all you. Money becomes an anchor around your neck, losing the love of another person becomes a weight on your chest that makes it hard to breathe, and work becomes an unfulfilling, slow death that you endure day in and day out. But the first step onto that path is to realize that, in any circumstance, we enter the arena a person capable of controlling just one factor: our response to the events around us. We can choose to feel whole before we are healed. We can choose to be loved before someone else loves us. We can choose purpose and meaning before the work we do offers it to us. Our emotional environment is the forcing function to create the change we want in life.

When I got back home from my shift that night after the *Call of Duty* suicide call, I stared up at my ceiling in the darkness, hands folded behind my head. The red shotgun shell was burned into my mind. It struck me that the patient was going to kill himself one way or the other. His method was most likely drugs because that was what he had available to him from his parents' supply. I wondered if he hoped that using drugs would send his parents a message from the grave. It was them that killed him. It was their habits, the years of their drug-induced negligence, that left him feeling alone and abandoned in the world. The shotgun and its accompanying shell, placed next to his bed, were just a backup. A contingency in case he woke up from the overdose and still needed to finish the job. Perhaps the video game he played was with the only friends he thought he had in the world. Maybe he had said goodbye to them as he pushed the plunger toward his arm and let the poison flow through him. He wasn't much older than me. He could have had a different life if he'd had better parents. He could have fought his demons if only he'd had a mentor to show him how.

When a tragedy unfolds, it's easy to assign blame. That young man's death was a tragedy, and I assigned the blame to his parents. Perhaps that was a fair assessment. But that doesn't change the fact that it was he who put the needle in his arm. He had planned so thoroughly to complete his suicide attempt that he left no possibility of failure. But what if? What if, in his darkest moment, there was one step more he had to complete—what if he'd called a friend? What if he'd had a mentor he could reach out to? Could someone have saved him?

Could someone have saved my friends?

Could I?

Rugby is an unforgiving sport, and they played a tough game well. When they got hit hard, they always had a hard hit ready to give back. I remember both of them on separate occasions playing through a game with a bloody injury. An errant elbow caught one above the eye, and the other took a head to his cheek that opened it up. Nothing in sports is more Viking-like than watching a player ask to get put back

CHAPTER 7

on the field, wild-eyed and smeared with blood, and make a tackle the next play. It's berserk. They played through bloody injuries and knew the difference between being *hurt* and being *injured*. But I guess somewhere inside they weren't just bloody and bruised. They were injured in ways they didn't let others see. There was a part of their soul they were losing every day that kept them from getting ready for their next match.

Hemingway was a combat veteran, war correspondent, successful author, and role model to many. The characters he wrote into creation reflected his personal experiences in combat and as an observer of the Spanish Civil War. The wisdom he offered the world through his novels emerged from the suffering he'd witnessed firsthand. But you can never be too tough, too experienced, or too manly to not give your mental health the level of seriousness it deserves.

If we don't want to open up authentically, it's easy to fool our classmates and teachers, bosses and coworkers, teammates and friends. They can't spot mental illness the way we can spot a patient enduring round after round of chemotherapy. From an early age, we learn to master our facade, the fake face we put on when we go out into public. We insolate ourselves from the questions and the unwanted prying of others with simple responses to how we are doing: "I'm fine, how are you?" We get the ball out of our court and into theirs as quickly as possible.

Perhaps your version of masculinity is to bear your struggles in silence. Maybe your version of femininity is that a woman is capable of handling all of her emotions. Maybe your version of a hero is that they will spend their time fighting external battles on the side of good against evil and would never have to fight the internal battle for their soul. But there will be a time in your life when you reach what you think is your limit. The military will bring you to the edge of your comfort zone and then push you past it. Writer's block will bring you to your knees. All-nighters studying for the MCAT or LSAT will turn you into a zombie. Life wants to break you down so that it can build you back up into something more powerful and more resilient than you were—and life *will* break every one of us, that's a promise. I hit my breaking point in my hotel room. My two teammates, Hemingway, and my patients all hit theirs in their own lonely places. What happens when we break? Just how low can one go without losing their will to live?

The moments when you find yourself at the end of your rope are when you learn that you have an internal reservoir of strength to draw from. Your heroic journey will take you on a lifetime of learning—you will face your shortcomings, you will fail, and you will experience gut-wrenching loss. What you do in those moments determines whether your story continues to be a hero's journey or becomes a deep tragedy. And make no mistake: your story cannot be lived alone. It doesn't matter if you are a man or a woman. If you are single or partnered. It doesn't matter if you bench press seven hundred pounds, and it doesn't matter if you have more money than Scrooge McDuck. If you are just one stick, you will break; but a bundle of sticks tightly bound holds great strength. We destroy mental health stigmas when we can talk honestly with each other, without fear of stigma or judgment. We develop resiliency with true friendships and deeper relationships.

When I was at my lowest point in that hotel room—eating like a glutton, drinking like a fish, dropping out of grad school, and ending my relationship—I had a choice to make: keep struggling alone and in silence or reach out to a lifeline. I chose the lifeline. I called my parents and told them everything. To my surprise, they weren't angry. They didn't scold me or shame me. My worst fears about how they would take the news never manifested. Before I ended the phone call, they told me they loved me. Despite the excess pounds hugging my waistline, I felt lighter than I had in as long as I could remember. I felt free.

Western Judeo-Christian values teach that people are fundamentally flawed. We have a propensity to sin, to miss the mark of perfection, and in our capacity for free will, we will intemperately choose to sin again and again. Redemption from that inherent flaw is an act of grace in the form of a sacrifice made by Jesus—the man least deserving of

CHAPTER 7

suffering chose the worst imaginable death so that our sins would be forgiven. Grace is a hard concept. It's difficult to forgive someone who has wronged you, but it's even harder to forgive yourself. We know when we aren't acting the way we should. That still-small voice in our heads and hearts doesn't let us get away with anything. So how can we get back onto the path we know we should be traveling? How do stop doing what we know we shouldn't do? I reached out for the grace of others. With one short phone call, I built momentum.

After I talked to my parents, I listened to a *Tim Ferriss Show* podcast where he interviewed an author who was almost the exact opposite of me. A liberal Massachusetts Buddhist, she most likely would not have approved of my warrior profession. But she was exactly what I needed. I owe her a debt of gratitude. Her name was Tara Brock, and she wrote a book called *Radical Acceptance*. Through her book and teachings, I learned how to meditate. I cleaned up the beer cans and recycled the pizza boxes. I went to the gym and ate the first vegetable I could remember in a long, long time. I started demonstrating the first forms of compassion toward myself that I could manage. I entered the self-care stage of self-help recovery, where her thought exercises finally healed some of my old teenage wounds.

As I pored over her book and reflected on her guidance, I realized I had never moved past the pain of not being able to save people. I had never come to terms with that loss of innocence. I began to piece my life story together and to stare into the spots where coping mechanisms had created blindness. How, like most men lost on their life's journey, I had used alcohol as a crutch. How hard I had worked to try to be good enough. How I had elevated saving someone else's life to become the equivalent of saving my own. How I had tried to become worthy of the love that I was unwilling to give myself by achieving goals and receiving praise from others.

I realized I had never forgiven myself. I had never allowed myself to feel the true pain of what it is to be a seventeen-year-old who just failed to save someone's life. I had never acknowledged the full force of the anger I felt for the parents who could callously watch their son be wheeled out of their house while only thinking about themselves. I had been running from pain. I had been hiding from guilt. I had been avoiding shame.

Finally, I could choose to close those chapters of my life and move into the next. Stoicism was the tool I wished I had as a younger person.

CHAPTER 8

HE IS A WISE MAN WHO DOES NOT GRIEVE FOR THE THINGS WHICH HE HAS NOT BUT REJOICES FOR THOSE WHICH HE HAS.

—EPICTETUS

Let me introduce you to some heroes. In my free time, I like to study history. It helps me understand my job in the Army better when I look to examples from the past of people who encountered similar problems and overcame them. Once, I stumbled upon a story of two legends that fought each other for thirty years using guerrilla tactics, or the ambush and raid tactic typical of American warfare. One man was French, the other a colonist born in Massachusetts. The following is only the story of the Frenchman and his descendants.

The young French soldier came to North America in 1665. His name was Jean-Vincent d'Abaddie de Saint-Castin, and he was a distant cousin of Artemis, one of the famed Three Musketeers. Jean-Vincent was thirteen when he went to war on the North American continent. That was the way of his time. As an ensign, he was the lowest-ranking officer in the army. By the time he turned eighteen, he was promoted to lieutenant and placed second in command of a fort along the Maine coastline called Pentagoet, where he fought Dutch pirates and English raiders. After one raid, he was captured and sent to Boston as a prisoner of war but escaped. To get back to French territory, he traveled through four hundred miles of enemy English and Iroquois lands until finally arriving in Quebec to be sent back to his fort in Maine.

Instead of returning home to France to inherit his father's lands and claim his noble title of Baron of Saint-Castin, he stayed and embedded himself into the Penobscot tribe. He would go on to fight the English for the next thirty years, becoming a war chief among the Abenaki people and continuing to look after their interests with the French government. He fought with them for their freedom. He married a war chief's daughter. They had a family, and his sons would be war chiefs and fight the English for decades after his death. His legacy and that of the tribe he helped save continued to be woven into the tapestry of American history.

One of Saint-Castin's descendants, Charles Norman Shay, earned France's highest medal for valor during World War II. As of this writing, he is ninety-seven years old and lives on Indian Island in Old Town, Maine. He is a Penobscot Indian tribal elder. But when he was much younger, Charles stormed the beaches of Normandy as a combat medic. What Charles did that day can never be summed up in words. Charles was one of the first Americans to land on D-Day, while German machine gunners poured devastating fire into his amphibious landing craft. In an interview Charles said "It was every man for himself" as the soldiers laden with seventy-five pounds worth of food, weapons, ammunition, and equipment plunged into the Atlantic waters and onto the beach.

The soldiers standing in front of his amphibious landing vehicle were cut down. Charles made it into the water. Between him and any relative cover was a quarter mile of sand. He bounded across the open kill zone of the enemy machine gunners and made it to a sand dune. There, dozens of soldiers had laid themselves down, exhausted from their sprint across the sandy beach. Without hesitation, Charles went to work performing his job as a combat medic. He treated anyone

CHAPTER 8

he could find, regardless of which unit they belonged to. Then, from his position of relative safety, Charles looked back to see a nightmare. Behind him, still exposed to withering enemy fire, wounded American soldiers were drowning in the surf. Exposing himself once again to death, he stood up under effective enemy fire and ran *toward* the ocean. Charles pulled soldier after soldier onto the beach and saved them from drowning. There, he found his friend, Private Edward Morozewicz, mortally wounded. Both men knew it would be the last time they would see each other alive. They said their goodbyes while bullets snapped past them, mortar and artillery shells exploded, and the cries of the wounded grew louder. Charles had more men to save, even if it couldn't be his friend. He did his best to save as many as he could, though he doesn't know how many he pulled from the waves. He worked himself to exhaustion. An infantryman later stated that he saw Charles "carry men that were much bigger than himself."

Charles was a man torn between worlds—between the fight for freedom across the sea and the bondage he and his people suffered at home. The Penobscot Indians from Old Town Maine weren't allowed to vote in state or federal elections. The Congress that had voted for the war and the draft that had forced him into the US Army never received a single vote from him, his family, or his tribe. But there he was. Saving men, saving soldiers, saving his friends and his comrades with absolute disregard for his own life. Later, he started a family, and went to war and survived again in Korea. He didn't ask for medals. He didn't want recognition. He did what he did because he was who he was—and some things worth doing need to be done.

Next, meet Adam Brown, a small-town boy who grew up in Arkansas during the 1980s and 1990s. He always loved to play sports and earned a spot on his college football team as a hard-nosed, tough son of a bitch. But Adam was looking for an adventure, and with the influence of a bad relationship, he was exposed to and became addicted to drugs. He stole from his parents. He alienated people who loved him the most. His long road to recovery wasn't easy, but one day he met a woman who loved him, held him to a higher standard, and refused to let him regress back to the habit that always seemed to be knocking at his door. They got married and had two children.

Adam joined the Navy, training his drug-wasted body into the fighting machine that the Navy SEALs wanted. He deployed in routine training missions until September 11, 2001, when everything changed. Year after year, Navy SEAL teams were deployed to grueling combat rotations, Adam included, in spite of losing his dominant eye in a training exercise. He simply learned to shoot with his one remaining eye. On one deployment, Adam was wounded when his Humvee rolled over and crushed his hand between its metal frame and the road. He recovered, and despite the odds, he passed SEAL Team Six selection against peers who didn't have his injuries.

Adam made the ultimate sacrifice during a deployment to Afghanistan. His teammates did everything they could to save him, to no avail. A year and a half later, a helicopter carrying his teammates was shot down, killing all of the passengers. When speaking about Adam's legacy to *Time* magazine's Eric Blehm, one of his teammates unknowingly spoke about his own death that would soon come: "I either want to die in combat, doing my job right now, or live till I'm ninety-eight years old and see my great, great grandkids . . . I don't want anything in between. None of us do. A warrior's death, you can't get any higher than that. It's horrible for the family, they don't want to hear that, but for us, the guys at our command, we're okay with it. That is our duty, the highest calling. And if that happens to you, you hope you are in the right frame of mind that you are okay with it. I have seen a lot of people go, not well. Had they been able to do another take on it, they would probably want it to go better. I remember everything else about Adam, but I will always remember the end. You know, your first impression lasts a relationship, and your last impression is with you forever. *Adam died well.*" Adam's story and the story of his teammates are chronicled in the book *Fearless: The Undaunted Courage and Ultimate Sacrifice of Navy SEAL Team SIX*

CHAPTER 8

Operator Adam Brown by Eric Blehm. It's a book worth reading if you want to learn about sacrifice.

Admiral James Stockdale is the American military's most famous stoic warrior philosopher. He gained an exceptional academic pedigree in philosophy from Stanford University and lived out his moral and ethical code as an officer in the United States Navy. When an enemy rocket slammed into his jet, forcing him to eject over hostile territory, he was quickly captured and transported to confinement in the infamous Hanoi Hilton, the communist North Vietnamese Prison Camp. He was the highest-ranking naval officer and one of the longest-held American POWs in Vietnam, spending more than seven years in captivity.

In his book, *In Love and War: The Story of a Family's Ordeal During the Vietnam Years,* Admiral Stockdale described his treatment as a POW. He was tortured. He was starved. He was denied basic medical care. He was denied communication with his family. He was put into isolation, meant to force the suffering of unnatural separation from human contact *for years*. After being tortured for the thirteenth time, he broke a window in his prison cell and used the glass to slash his wrists, afraid he would give up information that would harm his fellow Americans. That was his breaking point—he would rather be responsible for his own death than reveal information that would cause the deaths of his comrades.

But what the communists failed to understand was the power of his mind—he broke, but he didn't shatter. His resolve to resist his captors made them change their methods. He learned to lead other American POWs under inhumane treatment with firm guidance and unfailing commitment. And he endured those horrors and lived to see his wife and kids. Later, he went back to Vietnam and visited the prison where he had been tortured for the better part of a decade. He knew that he could leave captivity yet still remain in bondage to hate and resentment. He knew that he had the power to break free from the chains that place had put on him. Prison and torture gave him the love of liberty that inspired him to run for the second highest office in the free world, and he ran for vice president as an Independent candidate in 1992.

Senator John McCain came from legendary naval stock. His father and grandfather were seafaring men and American patriots whose leadership as admirals in World War II and Vietnam served our nation. When Lieutenant Commander John McCain was shot down, the communists quickly discovered his father's rank and tried to exploit him through propaganda. The enemy hoped to use the prestige of the McCain family to bolster their soldier's morale. In the book *Faith of My Fathers*, John McCain outlines his torture. He was denied treatment for his damaged leg and shoulder. He was only given enough food to slowly starve and waste away. When death was drawing near, his captors happily watching him slip further and further away from life, he was coerced into signing a letter that detailed things he didn't believe.

In his book, Senator McCain talks about the rebuilding process after torture. He knew he could have done better and resisted more. After all, who doesn't hold the crushing fear that our deepest and darkest shame will be revealed publicly; it's natural to keep sins hidden from the eye of others. The shame he felt from breaking is the shame we would all feel if we publicly sold out against our most dearly held beliefs. But no one is strong enough to withstand overt and unchecked evil. Everyone has a breaking point. Senator McCain gathered himself after that and resisted his captors until he was released at the end of the war. He came home, continued to serve the nation in the Navy until retirement, and became a US Congressman and Senator. He ran for President in 2008 as the Republican nominee. In those broken spots, he formed a new strength and then offered it to the world. Senator McCain was fond of one of the Shawnee war chief Tecumseh's famous quotes and repeated it often:

"So live your life that the fear of death can never enter your heart. Trouble no one about their religion; respect others in their view, and demand that they respect yours. Love your life, perfect your life,

CHAPTER 8

beautify all things in your life. Seek to make your life long and its purpose in the service of your people. Prepare a noble death song for the day when you go over the great divide. Always give a word or a sign of salute when meeting or passing a friend, even a stranger, when in a lonely place. Show respect to all people and grovel to none. When you arise in the morning give thanks for the food and the joy of living. If you see no reason for giving thanks, the fault lies only in yourself. Abuse no one and no thing, for abuse turns the wise ones to fools and robs the spirit of vision. When it comes your time to die, be not like those whose hearts are filled with the fear of death, so that when their time comes they weep and pray for a little more time to live their lives over again in a different way. Sing your death song and die like a hero going home."

Both Admiral Stockdale and Senator McCain remind us that, even when we break, we still have much to offer the world. They continued to serve our country despite having been crushed down to the depths of their soul. It's from those lowest moments that they found the strength to ascend to the highest peaks of their heroic journeys.

Travis Mills wrote a life-changing book called *Tough as They Come*, but before that he was a typical small-town American kid. Growing up in rural Michigan, in a town where everybody knew everybody, he stood out. He was always a large kid, and his size made him an asset on the football field. After playing in high school and a brief stint in college, Travis enlisted in the Army. The idea of jumping out of a perfectly good airplane seemed like the kind of future he wanted, so he joined the famous 82nd Airborne Division. He did two combat deployments, leaving his wife and newborn baby behind on his third and final tour to Afghanistan. By then, he had been promoted to staff sergeant and was responsible for leading his squad in combat. One day he placed his backpack down inside of a compound and unknowingly detonated an IED. The explosion made S.Sgt. Mills the fourth out of five US service members to become a quadruple amputee. He lost both of his arms and both of his legs.

The combat medic in his platoon saved his life initially and the flight crew medic continued to keep him alive in the medical evacuation helicopter. At each level of medical care in Afghanistan, Germany, and America, medical personnel saved his life over and over again. Within days of his injury, he arrived at Walter Reed—the same hospital that I received my beesting allergy injections from, and just one year afterward. He would spend months learning how to use his prosthetic limbs to relearn how to walk, how to eat, and how to live. Travis wrote that he struggled with his new body. Who wouldn't? In our wildest dreams we couldn't imagine having to live the rest of our lives without our limbs. But at twenty-four years old, and as the father to a seven-month-old daughter, that's what Travis had to contend with. His heroic journey had culminated in apparent tragedy.

I've had the honor to meet Travis. His personality fills a room. You might think you know someone like that, but you haven't met Travis. He brings the same magnetic energy into a room that he had before his wounds, but with refocused purpose and vigor. He found a new heroic path. He started a charitable organization that rehabilitates wounded veterans in the Maine wilderness. The same place where I found adventure, healing, and peace he now uses to bring forward the best inside men and women who were touched by war. His organization has even grown to participate in a Toy Drop charity event where his old unit, the 82nd Airborne, encourages its paratroopers to purchase toys that they pack into their rucksacks. The crazy jumpers then exit the plane with the toys safely stored away, then land on the drop zone where waiting children who would otherwise have a toyless Christmas watch the magic happen. Travis's heroic journey took him from warrior to leader and in a way, to healer. He shows wounded warriors the path to fulfillment—how to live a life at peace so that they can continue on their own journeys.

Men like Charles Norman Shay, Travis Mills, Adam Brown, Senator John McCain, and Admiral Stockdale match my definition of a hero, even though each of their actions and responses were unique. On your heroic journey, you might not go to war. You might not sacrifice your life. You might not be wounded or captured and tortured by your enemies. The actions that you take in your life will not have a crowd to witness them. No movie crew will follow you around in everyday life. You and I are just going to wake up each day and live it out as best as we can before we go to sleep. Day in and day out. It won't feel glorious. Few metrics will tell us if we are on track. We will grind and put our nose down and do the work and every now and then find some small satisfaction in what we have accomplished.

What is it that pulls you along on your journey? Do you want fame? Recognition? Do you want all of the perks that come with being the best in your craft and never having to worry about money again? Do you want to be worthy of love? Much of our conversation together has been centered on how we as individuals can become the best version of ourselves. But our true transformation doesn't happen until we see what good we can achieve for others. When you have become an artist who has their own exhibit, will you use your influence to help other struggling artists? When you've achieved what it is you want to achieve for yourself, can you see what remains to be done for others?

True work and proper progress happen in the shadows. Behind the curtain. Actors rehearse lines at home before they step on stage at the theater. Singers and musicians play in garages and sing in the shower before they perform in front of an audience. We work jobs from nine to five and spend precious moments of our free time working on our hobbies and passions. We are walking on our heroic journey when no one is looking, and we only have ourselves to answer to. When we become fixated on achieving our heroic vision in that way, we gain experience, and that's what allows us to give back to others. To share our experience with the next group of people coming behind us. We can take all the worst parts of the journey and process them into the lessons others will need.

Part of this maturation is coming to grips with the price we must pay to undertake that journey. Travis Mills paid the price with his body. Adam Brown paid with his life. POWs pay the price of years spent in confinement that they will never get back. Artists get evicted. Writers face endless rejection. Entrepreneurs go bankrupt. Even worse, you're not the only one who will be called to sacrifice, to suffer as you accomplish your calling. Your family and friends will pay the tax too. Military spouses run their families, often as single parent, while worrying that their spouse might not return from the deployment alive. Parents who encourage their children to develop their art do it knowing the pressure their child must be under to make something of themselves and get their big break. Friends drop their plans and come to each other's aid when their dreams are crushed and the pieces of a shattered future have to be put back together.

Dr. Peterson explains the concept of sacrifice as fundamental in the development of human civilization. The idea that present pain is worth future benefit radically changed human progress. Farmers could sweat and toil all day for weeks in a field so that one day the plants they took such diligent care of could be harvested, and the surplus of food could then last through a harsh winter. Conversely, Seneca wrote, "No man is more unhappy than he who never faces adversity. For he is not permitted to prove himself."

When you give up on something difficult you are doing now, you are losing who it is you might become in the future if you stick with it. And that's a sacrifice you shouldn't be willing to make. What's worse, if you don't experience the process of personal sacrifice to obtain the things you want in your own life, you don't develop the ability to recognize the sacrifices others have made for *you*. Free things sound nice. Free sounds generous. But nothing in this world is free. Not your education, not the food that you eat, and not the freedom you have to become who it is you want to be. Everything is cheapened—nothing has value because our effort has not paid the cost of ownership.

Still, it doesn't seem fair that we can try to do the right thing and be punished for it anyway. The reality of life strikes us as fundamentally unjust. If we do good, we should receive good. The outcomes of our

CHAPTER 8

efforts aren't guaranteed. Success isn't promised. Good people suffer along with the bad, and we are left wondering why.

This is because justice feels good to dish out—but it's often clouded by anger and rage. Our sense of justice is one of our most easily manipulated emotions. Have you ever replayed an argument in your head to get your words just right so that their biting effect is perfectly timed to cut the deepest, despite the fact the argument ended hours ago? The more things we are told to be angry and enraged about, the more we risk losing control of what is truly just. It also makes us incapable of engaging in deep, meaningful conversations with people who have opposing beliefs. Seneca wrote, "He who decides a case without hearing the other side, though he decides justly, cannot be considered just." True justice is a stoic virtue ruled by wisdom. Heroes don't look for the next opportunity to be offended by someone else; nor do they intentionally seek to offend others. As a hero, you are an agent of justice, and that's no idealistic or naive statement. It's important to have an ethically calibrated construct of good and evil, including the sacrifice justice requires.

The inner freedom we want, the lasting peace our souls crave, isn't found in a plush bank account or mansions or fame. If you want freedom, you have to learn to master yourself. Our bodies serve our minds, not the other way around. When was the last time you ran so far that your body cramped and your muscles froze stiff? Have you ever held a yoga pose past the point you initially thought you could? Or threw five extra pounds on the barbell and dug deep, past what you thought you were capable of? When the body experiences pain, it tells our minds to quit. To end the suffering, even if we are voluntarily doing to ourselves. Sometimes that natural response is life-saving, but without being tempered by courageous sacrifice, justice, and wisdom, it can keep you from learning the strength you have inside of you.

After the war, Charles Norman Shay built a good life for himself. But he never lost his eye for the forgotten. Sixty years later, he went back to Omaha Beach. This time, he wasn't a scared young man wondering if he would survive the desperate fight of D-Day. He felt that there was a chapter to his life that was not complete. He went to the same beach where he had said goodbye to his friend, and he performed a Penobscot tribal ritual meant to guide wandering spirits home. Charles worried that there were souls still on that beach, lost and unable to find their way into the afterlife. So he showed them the way home, in the way of his people, the only way he knew how.

Stoicism is a tool for those of us who want to make sure we can come home from one of our journeys. The teachings are quick sanity checks used to make decisions, even in morally ambiguous environments. Stoicism teaches us to remember that we only have one life to live, so we must use it to serve others and provide for our families. To not let other people rob us of joy—it is ours to give away, so we must guard it. Heal from pain, forgive what can be forgiven, and seek true justice for what is unforgivable. Break addictions, break old mindsets, and break the cycle of pain that we are capable of stopping in our own lives and in the lives of others.

CHAPTER 9

THE CAVE YOU FEAR TO ENTER HOLDS THE TREASURE YOU SEEK.

—JOSEPH CAMPBELL

Our heroic journey is initially a journey of self-discovery. When we are young, we wonder who we might become. We are unsure of ourselves, unconfident in our abilities, unsure what we are capable of. As we get older and gain more experience from life, if we are living out our heroic callings well, a shift occurs. It is no longer a self-centered quest; we mature into our journey by making it about other people. When you've learned enough about yourself from the obstacles on your journey, you'll find there will be more of you now to share with the uninitiated. You will have learned lessons, earned money, made connections, and gained wisdom. But the line between becoming the hero of our lives or the villain of our lives is razor thin—and it's a margin that we all walk. We can be the masters of our journey or the masters of our destruction.

Some of us are reckless, especially when we're young. We sleep around, drink too much, and do hard drugs to feel something different from everyday life. Some of us isolate ourselves, barring the outside world with forcefields we erect from behind the locked doors of our bedrooms and the video games we play all night. Sometimes we hurt those we love with our words and actions. There will be times in our lives when we do something that we know should not be repeated. It might not be criminal, it might not be illegal, and it might not harm anyone else. But if you know inside your chest that what you did should not be done again, that is your conscience telling you to listen. If we abandon our conscience, our heroic path will divert at the intersection of the villain's journey.

For as much as I always wanted to be the hero, I know what it feels like to be the villain. And it happened so quickly. It was the winter of my sophomore year of college, and it was snowing. I was driving my little stick-shift sedan from my college to my family's house in Maine. It had been a long semester, and I wanted to be home and spend time at my cabin in the winter. My grandfather, my hero, had died a few months earlier. Losing a source of wisdom in your life is tough. The death of parents or grandparents means that we must become the source of wisdom they once were for us. They didn't teach me how to grieve in college. I didn't know what to do but escape into the solitude of winter from inside a woodstove-heated cabin. The two-lane highway twisted and turned into back country roads. The solid yellow lines faded under a gentle dusting of white powdered flakes. Fewer and fewer drivers seemed willing to brave the winter conditions on the road. But I had to get home.

As I rounded a corner, the driver of the car in front of me slammed on their brakes. I did as well. Only nothing happened. My foot punched the pedal, but it only groaned as the frozen brakes locked without slowing my speed. I swerved into the oncoming lane, still blind to any traffic coming around the bend, until the flashing lights of an ambulance came into view.

I tried to get back into my lane, but it was too late. The ambulance hit my front bumper and slid into the ditch on the side of the road.

"Tell me you don't have a patient in the back!" I yelled, exiting my car and into the snowstorm.

CHAPTER 9

"Yeah, we do," came the reply.

"Let me help!" I said, walking toward the ambulance a dozen yards away from me.

"Don't come any closer," the driver said. "The patient is fine, and we don't need any more of your help."

If it had been my ambulance, I doubt that I would have said anything different. The driver was stressed out from the call on bad road conditions and didn't have any patience left for me.

My old friend adrenaline had already shown up. My heart raced inside my chest. I stood shivering in the snow and waited for the police to show up. When they did, I got the distinct impression that they didn't like me. I was the driver that had hit an ambulance. I didn't like me either. The shame was unbearable. I had just done the unimaginable. The unspeakable. This was the antithesis of who I was. I was a former EMT—the guy who responded to accidents. I wasn't the guy who caused accidents, and I certainly wasn't the guy who hit an ambulance with a patient in the back. But there was no escaping it. I was responsible for the traffic jam forming behind us. I was responsible for the additional suffering the patient felt.

Another ambulance showed up and took the patient to the hospital. The ambulance I hit remained in the ditch. The police took their report. Half of the front bumper was ripped off my sedan and the front hood was dented and compressed upward. Me, my car, and my broken pride limped the rest of the way to Maine.

I didn't drive for the rest of my winter break. I didn't want to. The car needed to be fixed, and so did I. I beat myself up for days. I called myself every name in the book. Who hits an ambulance? What kind of person does that? The only answer I had was that *I was that person*. All the good I had done as an EMT felt like it had been wiped away in that moment. The scales tipped irreparably downward, showing me how flawed I really was.

I had built an identity around being a good guy, but the accident forced me to look at myself in a new light. I had to choose—either wallow in self-deprecating shame or extend myself a small element of grace. Accidents happen. And yes, some accidents are avoidable. But that only meant I could learn from what happened. I could plan my routes on bigger highways, check the weather before I left, plan to pull off at a restaurant and let the storm pass. I could purchase a vehicle that handles better in inclement weather.

In stoicism, there is a concept of *premeditatio malorum*, which translates to "a premeditation of evils." It acts as a guide to troubleshooting our plans. In the military, it is called war-gaming, but the concepts are the same. Take a plan and look at the weak points. Prepare for the worst so that what is avoidable is avoided, and you'll know that whatever complications inject themselves into the situation truly were uncontrollable factors. There is risk in every decision we make. There are consequences for our actions that have second- and third-order effects. There are an infinite number of factors to consider before making any decision, and there are an infinite number of consequences that come from the actions we take. Even our best-laid plans don't survive first contact with the enemy.

No one is perfect, so when we err, we can either take responsibility or hide our guilt. Blame points the finger away from us and toward people who did nothing wrong. In my accident, I could have blamed the person driving in front of me. Why did they slam on their brakes and force me to do the same? There was no reason for that. And why was the ambulance driver driving so fast that he couldn't brake properly either? It could have been my school's fault for holding me in class so late that I had to leave right in the middle of the storm instead of missing it like I had planned. Why hadn't the transportation department plowed the road like it was their job to do?

Villains thrive on blame. I became the villain of my life by blaming myself incessantly with no path to forgiveness. The line between taking responsibility and negative self-talk requires wisdom to navigate. Taking personal responsibility is a process that leads you to reconciliation. It keeps you from staying trapped in the shame cycle.

Villains can also orient blame onto others. They build an internal reservoir of resentment that transfers onto innocent people. And most of us, at some level, can relate. A compelling villain in any movie or novel is someone we can identify with. Relatable. Someone who has been touched by the tragedy of life and has consciously molded themselves into someone capable of overcoming it. Except instead of building their internal resolve in the hope of one day helping others, they survive their past only to torment others in the future. To be wholly and monstrously evil makes a character one-dimensional. And that's not how it works in real life either. No world leader who has committed genocide has effectively started their process of evil by overtly explaining their plan from day one. They build a following, and they craft messages that maximize disgust and fear. And when their base of support is emotionally ready, they strike. The villain inside them has its time in the sun.

My definition of achieving maturity is realizing that the greatest challenge we will encounter is ourselves. When you investigate your shadow, you realize how fragile things are around you. It is easier to destroy than it is to create; easier to burn a building down than to build one. To be a doctor or nurse takes years of learning in order to save lives, but in one moment a life can be snuffed out. What is good and noble takes time to generate. It takes consistent, persistent effort to accomplish something of value and to offer it as a benefit to others. The culminating difference between a hero and a villain is in who they serve. A hero starts the journey hoping to be the best version of themself, but transitions into becoming better and better so they might serve others. A villain gathers influence only to wield it in whatever manner they please, and it won't matter at whose expense.

Carl Jung was a Swiss psychiatrist who developed several theories about archetypal behaviors—physiological patterns of behavior that people tend to follow at various stages of their lives and are manifested in their personality. Jung also expanded on the idea of the shadow. Part of becoming a more powerful, more integrated being is to understand the destruction you are capable of unleashing on others and on yourself. This encounter with the shadow destroys the naive idea that we are only good. That we could never and would never do anything to harm someone else. A docile woman and a nice guy aren't inherently good, because in order to be good there must be an ability to resist bad. A good man is a dangerous man who has the dark side of his persona under lock and key. A good woman is a lioness who knows exactly how to defend her pride. Until we encounter our shadow and understand it, we are naive to whatever villain we encounter.

We all have a shadow in us, and if we don't conquer our own, we become vulnerable to someone else's. Villains are masters of the shadows in others. A villain validates the anger we feel. There is a deep resonance with outrage and frustration that things aren't the way that they should be, and when someone finally says those things, we hear the truth in their words and miss the deception in their actions. What is the end state that someone who uses our outrage and anger wants to accomplish?

When heroes encounter their shadows, they learn the true power they have within them. They can be cruel, they can be savage, and they can be anything that has ever harmed another person. They are not exempt from being forces for evil simply because they don't think they're evil people. A hero must learn how to control that power. Anger is one of the shadow's tools that can lead us to unintentionally harm people in our lives. Anger is seductive. It lures us into thinking we are justified, that our indignation is righteous and therefore our cutting words or scathing self-talk are authorized.

After the accident with the ambulance, I was angry with myself. I should have known better and done things differently. But by stewing and brewing on my actions, I brought them from the past and relived them in my present. I fixated on the things I did wrong instead of acknowledging them and moving on. Negative self-talk keeps us from gleaning what wisdom there is to learn from a mistake so that we can avoid it in the future. All that anger we feel makes us primed to become

CHAPTER 9

the villain of our lives. Our past is a record that helps us anticipate the future, but if we can't put it behind us, our mistakes follow us into the present and create opportunities to repeat themselves. There is an appropriate amount of shame that we should feel when we err because we need to engage in reflection to extract meaning from events in the past. But the goal and aim of our internal examinations shouldn't end with burning ourselves at the stake.

The problem with anger is that it stems from our belief that things should be different from what they currently are. Sometimes anger is justified, but more often than not, our anger stems from our desire to blame someone else for our unhappiness. Stoicism teaches us that our anger is controllable. We get angry when someone makes a joke at our expense. We are frustrated when the teacher assigns too much homework. We lose our composure when life seems unfair. Stoicism encourages us to pause in those moments, to realize that we are reacting to what is happening around us. Marcus Aurelius wrote, "You shouldn't give circumstances the power to rouse anger, for they don't care at all."

Stoicism breaks down life into two major categories: what we can control and what we cannot control. Plato wrote, "There are two things a person should never be angry at: what they can help, and what they cannot." If we are angry about things we cannot control, we are wasting our time. If we are angry about things we can control, we are wasting our time being angry instead of fixing the problem and finding a solution. Epictetus taught, "To achieve freedom and happiness, you need to grasp this basic truth: some things in life are under your control, and others are not. What things are under your total control? What you believe, what you desire or hate, and what you are attracted to or avoid."

This sense of control can only come from wisdom—the virtue that governs courage, temperance, and justice. Like in *Lord of the Rings*, it's the one ring made to rule them all. Wisdom helps you decide when a courageous show of force is needed or when temperate judgment is the better course of action. Wisdom is the process of allowing past experiences to shape current decisions. It is the tool you need to weigh the difference of opinions in the world. To measure wars as worthy of your service or not. It sifts through the propaganda and the lies like a search filter in your email inbox. Wisdom gives you the confidence that what you believe is right without allowing anger to send you into bigotry or fundamentalism. Wisdom manages the middle ground of temperance and allows for a case-by-case allocation of justice. Wisdom keeps you from being seduced by your lesser self, and wisdom grows in direct correlation to your ability to feel compassion. Wisdom is the antidote to naivete.

If you are young, chances are you have already lived the experiences that will one day make you wise. Already, if you examine your past properly, you can unlock the lessons screaming at you, dying to be learned. If you've already suffered and endured, you have a gift to offer yourself. But only if you are willing to take the time to heal with proper introspection. It takes an element of wisdom to understand what you are personally capable of. That you contain within you all the tenacity of the heroic spirit. That you have endurance and grit locked within you that you don't even know you are capable of. You can run faster and longer, work harder, learn more, and love better than you currently are. And the counterbalance of all that goodness within you is the capacity for the opposite. If you have no awareness of the bad you are capable of, you'll find yourself embodying it, unaware of its power, kicking those around you to get what you want. You can become a bully just as easily as the bully did.

In high school, I had to read some books that I wouldn't have otherwise chosen, and many that I didn't particularly enjoy. But one I found interesting in spite of its old age was *The Iliad*. In the book, Achilles embodies the out-of-control and angry warrior. No one could stand up to his wrath because he was the best warrior on the battlefield. He is also the king of smack talk and has the kill count to back it up. But Achilles makes bad choices. He quarrels with his boss and allows his pride to keep him from fighting with his fellow Greeks. In his place, his best friend (or cousin) Patroclus takes Achilles's armor, puts it on, and leads his fellow countrymen to fight against the Trojan hero Hector. Patroclus dies leading the men Achilles should have led, literally becoming the empowering image Achilles should have been. Achilles responds to his cousin's death by embarking on a one-man crusade of vengeance that leads the Greek army to rape, pillage, and burn the city of Troy out of existence. Achilles vents his rage, draining every last ounce of blood lust out of him as he dies from Paris's well-placed arrow shot. The lesson we learn from the story is that the effects of our anger often lead to second- and third-order effects—unintended consequences that only make the situation much worse.

The military uses rules of engagement to make sure that violence doesn't rampage into the lives of innocent people. These guidelines are a modern attempt to contain the rage of Achilles inside the fighting men and women of our nation. But Western media has learned that "if it bleeds, it leads," and that sensationalized stories will make them money. They have learned that, with a big enough audience, they can call anything truth and have it become so. Stoics have to set their own rules of engagement. They are always looking for what is happening behind the scenes and questioning the legitimacy of propaganda and disinformation. A hero and a stoic learn not to be manipulated by other people's emotions.

We often think of people who are the angriest as the people who care the most about social issues. Why else would they be in such a state of emotional upheaval if things around them weren't in a state of crisis? There is such a thing as righteous indignation. Chances are, though, that what you think is a just and true sense of outrage is really just your pride getting hurt or your sense of ego getting offended. There's a balance between identifying what is dangerous (therefore a just sense of anger) and what is offensive (a matter of pride and ego being offended). Marcus Aurelius had plenty of opportunities to become angry and to vent his entire rage on the objects of his displeasure. Cooks, servants, advisers, generals, politicians, and the mob were helpless to stop the power of the emperor if they fell out of his favor. But instead of assuming that he was always correct and had the right to throw an imperial temper tantrum, he did a little thinking and a little philosophizing.

Marcus Aurelius had to solve the problems of his empire—after all, he was the boss—and not problems he created. He wrote, "A real man doesn't give way to anger and discontent, and such a person has strength, courage, and endurance—unlike the angry and complaining." Instead of getting angry when he had to fix other people's mistakes, he got to work with a cool and level head. "The nearer a man comes to a calm mind, the closer he is to strength." What is worse is that the team around him didn't always help him solve the issues of the empire. Every morning he would wake up and tell himself, "The people I deal with today will be meddling, ungrateful, arrogant, dishonest, jealous and surly. They are like this because they can't tell good from evil. But I have seen the beauty of good and the ugliness of evil and have recognized that the wrong doer has a nature related to my own."

Have you seen the beauty of good? How long is your fuse before it detonates on those around you? When other people make you angry, have you forgotten the times when you did that very thing to someone else that is now bothering you? On your heroic journey, there will be trials and battles where you have to plant your feet in the ground and face your foe. But when you look at the world and all the different people and ideas that are in it, it's important to remember that not everyone is your enemy. Anger feels good when we justly get to orient it at the villains of the world. Yet once we are head down, charging blindly along with the rest, we have surrendered our individual sovereignty.

When I first started lifting weights, I wanted to get stronger. I wanted to get huge muscles and look good at the beach with my shirt off. As I got older, I started working out for a different reason. I didn't care so much about aesthetics. I cared more about functional fitness for my job. I needed stamina and strength in my legs, which meant I couldn't skip leg day for the third week in a row. It meant I had to

CHAPTER 9

treat my body like it was a resource that needed to be taken care of. It needed more than just strength; it needed flexibility and stability to create longevity. I learned to care less about the immediate results and more about the long-term benefits of physical training.

Anger is the arm day of your mind: one thousand bicep curls later, your pump will look good and feel great. But are you really stronger for it? Anger gets us pumped up and ready to go, but has your anger ever solved a problem in your life?

Staying calm when everyone around you is outraged and irrationally engaging in mob behavior is difficult. When it comes to living a principled life, what comes easiest is often the wrong answer. It's easier than you think to be tricked into disliking someone for silly reasons. Ads, news articles, tweets, social media posts, and even books are written with the hope of getting a reaction from you. Clickbait is calculated, systematic propaganda aimed at manipulating you. Seneca reminds us we must check our first impulse to outrage: "In order that each man may be the more watchful and keep a careful eye on himself, do you not want me to point out that, though other vile passions affect only the worst sort of men, anger creeps up even on enlightened men who are otherwise sane?"

Sometimes anger and fear intermix into the same emotional state and are hard to separate. Fear is useful. Fear can keep you alive. But fear, when directed toward the wrong people or ideas, is a bad thing. Fear of getting hurt can cause us to close ourselves off to love so we don't experience another heartbreak. Fear of yet another public failure keeps us from embarking on the adventure of our life. Fear can keep us from driving because we don't want to cause another wreck. Fear paralyzes us into inaction and traps us into adopting a pessimistic worldview.

If you haven't spotted the parts of your shadow that would cause you to stampede with a herd, then you won't know if you are running in fear because everyone else is scared around you. Encountering your shadow keeps you from being blinded by fear.

Stoicism encourages us to take a step back and look at life from the balcony view. Stoics try to create separation between what they *think* and what they *feel*. We can become less reactionary when we can expand the time that occurs from thought to action. We can make fewer angry mistakes when we pause and allow for compassion to stop us from yelling at someone who isn't at fault. We can solve more problems if we take a strategic view and don't get pulled into the battlefield of outrage.

There will be times on your journey when you will be wronged. There will be times when you wrong others. The pathway to forgiveness and redemption is an internal one that everyone has to figure out how to balance. Heroes can offer grace and mercy to themselves and those around them, and by choosing that over blame will remain on their hero's journey. Villains blame others. And villains will try to inspire shame and guilt within you that isn't true.

Knowing what not to do what not to be is a helpful guide rail to keep you on track. If you don't have a crystal-clear vision of what you want to become, and equally as important, if you don't have a crystal-clear vision of what you *don't* want to become, you are vulnerable to becoming anything. If you don't know what being the best parent possible looks like for you, then slipping into mediocrity is easy. If you don't know what your exact fitness goals are, then your body slips into complacency. If you don't have certain behaviors preidentified that you would never do, then you might do anything for a promotion or fame. Few cheaters start relationships planning to cheat on their partner.

If you feel as if you know everything, I would caution you. Mastery takes time. Academics take a decade to get a doctorate. Professional athletes spend their entire lives honing skills. Artists are always looking to improve their craft. Businessmen and women constantly learn to adapt to changing markets. If you find yourself thinking that within your brilliance you have uncovered all there is to know, you create a blind spot for the shadow to grow. An illusion of mastery arrives and takes its place. But wisdom is a life-long pursuit. It calls us back over and over again. The wise life—the hero's life—is one in pursuit of

CHAPTER 9

the questions, finding new answers. Not so rigid that the shadow can dominate, and not so reckless that the shadow can rule in secret. There is an appropriate level of vigilance we need, preventive medicine, to keep ourselves from being led astray from the heroic journey that we are on.

CHAPTER 10

YOU ACT LIKE MORTALS IN ALL THAT YOU FEAR, AND LIKE IMMORTALS IN ALL THAT YOU DESIRE.

—SENECA

Stoicism is a philosophy for the trenches. It's a philosophy for the ERs and hospitals that save lives every minute of every day. It's a philosophy for the people who have been dealt trauma and have to figure out a way to keep on living in spite of their hurt. Stoicism is a reminder that life isn't fair, that the good suffers with the bad, and that inner peace is found when we focus on what is controllable and surrender to fate what is not. Learning from stoics has helped me prepare for training in austere conditions. It's helped me create inner endurance to deal with financial pressures and heartbreaks. I believe it has helped me be a better leader. I know it's helped me regain the range of spiritual motion that the scar tissue of life had degraded.

Part of my scar tissue is riddled with car wrecks, the events seared into my mind that I've encountered as an EMT and as a civilian. I've told you about motorcycle crashes and road rash. About my friend who broke her pelvis lying in the middle of the road. About how I was responsible for the crash with an ambulance, and how I struggled

CHAPTER 10

to come to grips with my actions unintentionally harming another person. But there is one more crash that I witnessed that I haven't told you about. This one is different. It happened five years after my friend the French monk introduced me to stoicism. And this crash was different because I was different.

It was a beautiful Maine summer day. I had awoken early to see the sunrise at 4:15a.m. in Acadia National Park. I watched the lobstermen sail out into the Atlantic Ocean as I swung in my hammock, eating a Jetboil breakfast and sipping on hot coffee, totally alone, and totally at peace. Later that morning, I went for a seven-mile run along the jagged coastline. When it was time to leave, I changed into sandals, put on some lightweight hiking pants and a moisture-wicking T-shirt, and made the drive up the coast to my family cabin in the woods. The drive was beautiful, taking me through sleepy coastal towns and rural villages. One intersection changed all of that—a Ford Explorer was upside down in the grass to the side, and since I wasn't a local, I had no idea how long the vehicle could have been in that position. It could have been abandoned. But something didn't feel right.

I pulled off onto a dirt road that led through a farmer's field and stepped out of my maroon Volkswagen Jetta. The grass draped over onto my unprotected feet with each step I took toward the wrecked SUV. The eerie calm was disrupted by a kid army crawling through a shattered window and out of the upside-down vehicle. *Game on*, I thought. My body knew what to do. Adrenaline surged like water released from an open dam. I sprinted the remaining 100 meters to the wreck as I watched the kid limp toward a man on the opposite side of the SUV. The man sat the boy down on his car's bumper and asked the kid a question.

When the man looked up, he saw me running toward him and pointed toward the wreck and shouted, "There's a mother and baby still inside!"

I didn't want to see what I was about to find. I ducked my head inside of the car and shuffled in through what had been the back window of the SUV. Every window was broken, and glass stabbed at my toes as I moved toward the middle row of seats.

My mind felt scattered, but being a first responder is about establishing order out of chaos. I remembered to start small and work up from there, and the old mental checklist that I had from my EMT days came back to me.

I was grateful to see the car seat had worked; the baby only looked to have minor injuries despite a gnarly head wound.

Was everyone breathing? Check.

Was there massive hemorrhaging? No.

He was bleeding though, and the salty taste of his own blood trickling into his mouth was unfamiliar to him. He didn't understand why he was lying sideways inside a rolled car. He was screaming in pain and anger, which added more stress and more adrenaline to the situation. From inside, I heard additional people gather around the wreck. Someone screamed "I smell gas!" and my stomach dropped.

A strong guy who looked like he earned his living with some sort of manual labor pried open the door with its broken frame, wedging his body in the space between the door and the car. Another guy entered the SUV and said what we all feared: "This wreck might blow!"

"Check for smoke!" I called out to a man who said he saw gas leaking.

I wanted to get out of that damned wreck, but we had to get the baby and the mother out too.

"Are you hurt?" I asked the mother in the driver's seat.

"I don't think so," came a dazed reply.

"Listen to me! Don't move your head. Starting from your toes and working your way to the top, try to move your body, little by little. Let me know what hurts." While the mom ran herself through a hasty triage, my priority was the baby. I wanted to keep the mom calm and have her working on a simple task so that she didn't start to panic.

Slow is smooth; smooth is fast. It was a military mantra that I silently chanted as my fingers searched for the buckle that would free the car seat.

"I need a knife!" I yelled to no one in particular.

CHAPTER 10

I was lying on my side on the glass, trying to find an angle to reach around and unbuckle the car seat. I paused and wiped blood away from the baby's eyes, which seemed to calm him down a bit.

"Thanks for the patience, little man," I said as I continued my hunt for the hidden buckle.

We had to keep the baby in the car seat because if he was hurt, it could be the only thing keeping his little broken body together. The whole thing had to come out.

I started to smell the leaking gas.

"I need a knife!" I said again.

A little pocketknife, no larger than half of my pinky appeared. But that little blade was sharp, and it cut through the seat belt with no trouble at all. I held the car seat in place as the tension released, then passed the car seat up to the man wedged between the body of the car and the door that wanted to shut. With a mighty push, I watched him shove the door off himself and pull the baby up and free of the wreck with his other arm.

Now it was time for the mom. She was overweight and struggling to pull herself free of the steering wheel. I wrapped my arms under her armpits as best as I could and pulled. But she was still stuck.

"You're going to have to work your legs free," I said, sweat starting to run into my eyes as the heat of the afternoon cooked the SUV.

"I can't," she said.

"Are you injured?" I asked, confirming again that she wasn't.

"No. But I just can't," I heard the defeat in her voice.

It would take strength to push herself up with her arms, giving her space enough to try and push off the ground with one leg so that the other could wiggle its way from under the steering wheel. She either had to try and free herself or we would have to wait for EMS to extract her with the jaws of life. The leaking gas suggested we should get out as fast as possible. I wasn't going to leave her, but I knew we might not have time to wait for help. The car could start burning, and it would be a good idea to not be inside when that happened.

"Listen to me," I said with an edge in my voice, fighting back the panic of being inside a metal box that was leaking gasoline. "We've got to get out of here. I can pull you free, but you have to get your legs free first. We *can* do this."

She gave it another try. I watched her push her body up with her arms, push off with one leg, and twist the other free. I pulled her out of the front seat and together we exited the car through the back window. Rubbernecking cars slowly passed us by. I was struck by the humanity of one offer, mother to mother, as a woman stopped her truck, her own baby crying in the backseat, and asked the mother if she needed diapers for her baby. The shared love for their children connected them, despite being total strangers. Now out of immediate danger, I looked around at the scene and was blown away. Five people had gathered to help us extract the family and were now taking care of the kid and baby, offering snacks and taking them into the shade. Downeast Mainers are good people to have around in an emergency. Without any training and without any hesitation, ordinary people became heroes.

As soon as EMS arrived, they treated the family and packaged them up to go to the hospital. Then the rest of us bystanders drifted toward our cars and went on our way. I never saw any of them again. I don't know what happened to the family after they left the scene. I hope that the little boy who army-crawled out of the wreck is okay. I hope the baby doesn't have a scar on his head. I hope the mother never takes for granted the gift that it is for her two children to be alive.

For me, the circumstances were no different from the many I had encountered as an EMT. I never got to know the ending. I never had closure as a teenage EMT. But as a man responding to a need, I realized that I was a different person in this scenario than I was when I was sixteen, seventeen, eighteen years old. A little more calloused. A little more experienced. But more than my age, I had matured. I had developed a stronger personal philosophy.

I knew, in retrospect, that no lives were really in danger in that wreck as long as the gas didn't ignite. Only some pain and suffering

CHAPTER 10

lurked there; not death. But in high school it took me a while to recognize when death was coming for someone. Medical calls were the hardest because the process of the body shutting down is an internal one; at least trauma calls had physical evidence, like blood, to gauge the severity. At the end of my time in EMT work, I needed the never-ending loop of getting a severe call, rising to the occasion, saving a life, then returning to wait for the next one. I needed bigger and bigger calls to feel like my efforts contributed to the larger balance, until an interesting thing happened. I lost track of those who I helped. Eventually, there were only the memories of those I didn't save, all crowded to the front of my mind. I had completely forgotten about calls where people were helped.

One such call came the Saturday night before my senior year of high school started. There was a tropical cyclone rolling up the East Coast. In a testament to the volunteer EMS and firefighter community around our country, our fire station was full of crews when the storm hit. Instead of being with their families, members of the community showed up to man the fire trucks, rescue engines, SWIFT water rescue boats, and ambulances. Wives cooked food and brought it in for everyone to share. An outside observer would have thought it was a neighborhood potluck and not a firehouse waiting to respond to the impending calls we knew would come during the storm.

The storm raged. The power went out. Our generators turned on. The radio started getting busy as calls came in. Crews started pushing out, getting wet in the rain, doing it all without earning a cent or getting paid a dime. They cleared debris from roads, helped people who had trees fall onto their homes, and came back to dry off and wait until their turn to head back out into the storm.

Then a cryptic medical call came in. A man called 911 and said he couldn't breathe. He only got out his address before then the phone went silent.

My crew spun up. Lou had responded to a fire call, so another driver stepped up to drive me and Jon to the address. The rain beat down on the ambulance so hard we couldn't hear the wail of the siren over the raging storm or read the numbers on the sides of the houses as sheets of rain came down. I walked up to a few house doors, then we found the house and knocked.

No one came to the door. We opened it and called out, "EMS! Did someone call 911?"

A noise came from the living room.

We found the man slumped in a chair. He was an older man, late fifties, overweight, with an oxygen tank next to him. Rubber tubing came from the tank and ran up and around his face, with little hooks blowing oxygen into each nostril.

He was barely conscious, and his blood oxygen level was in the eighties, so we hooked him up to our fresh tank of oxygen. A supervisor showed up—by then I knew that whenever he showed up the call was serious. I helped lift the patient onto the stretcher and out we rolled into the storm. Once inside the ambulance, the supervisor tossed me the keys to his SUV.

"Drive my vehicle to the hospital. We'll meet you there."

"Take it slow," Jon said. "We've got the patient, no need for you to get into a wreck."

Jon gave me a thumbs-up as I shut the back doors, and the ambulance took off.

I drove through the driving rain, following after the ambulance. The roads were deserted. Water pooled on the side of the streets as storm drains bubbled because they couldn't evacuate the rain in time. We met up at the hospital, the patient was wheeled away into the ER, and then Jon and I headed back to the station.

Everything ended well, as far as I know. A man who couldn't breathe and wouldn't have survived the night was taken to the hospital before he died in the middle of a tropical cyclone. We rode out the rest of the storm, and a few days later, I started my senior year of high school. But instead of putting this call into my memory bank of "jobs well done," it found its way into the background and remained buried for almost a decade.

CHAPTER 10

The whole concept of saving a life is complex. The highest standard for saving a life is when someone flatlines and then is brought back to life through the use of automated external defibrillators and adrenaline. But there are many times when someone is at death's doorstep and the result would be inevitable without intervention—but proximity to death is difficult to decipher. It doesn't always register that someone was saved. Furthermore, as a team, everyone works together to save someone. Our efforts were combined, and success was shared among us, not that there was ever a celebration.

Some achievements leave room to celebrate. When we graduate from high school, trade school, or college. When we get married. When we buy a home. When we pass a selection or achieve something professionally that few are capable of. In these moments we find ourselves standing on the mountaintop. We have conquered our goal; we have achieved what we have set out to accomplish. It's worth pausing in those moments, feeling that sense of accomplishment as the reward for the years of striving. Even better, pause to thank those in your life who supported you along the way.

Because once that feeling of success fades, you are left holding the bag for a now-empty purpose. You find that you are the same person, just with a new title. Awards and praise do little to change the internal dialogue we have with ourselves. We aren't magically made to feel whole or complete after we get what we want. The goal itself was the golden standard to which we measured our behavior. It provided structure, it gave us motivation, and it pointed out the direction we needed to go in life. But the heroic journey does not culminate in the worldly success we achieve. There isn't a title worth the price of the journey. We don't "make it," and we don't arrive at fulfillment through achievement. The journey itself is where we can find joy. It's not just about what we can become; it's about what we can become for other people.

But if our identity is intertwined with external metrics of success, we will always chase the trophy. Achievements will never be enough. It's why professional athletes who have accomplished the pinnacle of success in their sport don't retire at the top of their game. One Super Bowl ring isn't enough. One World Series win isn't enough. One time on top isn't enough if being on top is all the subsistence a journey has. This is not a knock on exhausting our potential and giving it our all, all the way until the end. It is a caution that we *will* spend our time and energy on accomplishing our version of success. If we don't know what enough feels like, there will always have to be another goal, another school, another million dollars to make. If we only measure our heroic journey in terms of individual accomplishment, the bar will keep rising.

As a soldier, the temptation is to believe that combat will be the fulfillment of your life, that within the danger, glory, camaraderie, and righteous cause of war, a soldier's heroic journey is complete. In some cases, that's true. But plenty of combat-hardened veterans have come back from war only to kill themselves. If we have accomplished all it seems there is to do in life, and life has struck a few blows in return, then our initial heroic calling seems devoid of purpose. And that void leads brave men and women to ending their life's journey early.

If you join the military, you will learn about formations. They will be the bane of your existence. In the military, the formation is a symbol of conformity. Dozens of people stand exactly the same way, wearing exactly the same thing, in organized rows and columns. Often, formations are used to organize soldiers for mass inspections. Your face will be examined for any unshaved hair. A single smudge on your uniform will be disastrous. If your weapon is inspected and carbon residue is left in the star chamber, your soul is immediately damned straight to hell in one of Dante's infamous layers. A formation enforces conformity to standards, to act as the policing function of the chain of command and to make sure orders are obeyed. Formations make everyone the same.

There's one formation we can learn a lot from. In the book *Ordinary Men: Reserve Police Battalion 101 and the Final Solution in Poland,* Christopher Browning chronicles a haunting scene that took

CHAPTER 10

place more than eighty years ago. On July 13, 1942, the battalion commander of the 101 Reserve Police Battalion, an Order Police unit based out of Hamburg, Germany, brought his men together into a formation. It was early in the morning; the men were bleary-eyed and hungry because they started their movement to the outskirts of the Polish village of Jozefow around 2 a.m. They wanted coffee, rest, and chow. Instead, the policemen gathered in an informal half-circle, a more intimate style of formation that brought the men closer to their leader.

Standing in front of them was the familiar sight of Major Wilhelm Trapp. They called him Papa Trapp as a term of endearment for the leader who had guided them through months of their deployment. The men in formation had been picked second by their nation because of their age or their civilian police background. They weren't drafted into the army or allowed to enter the prestigious corps of the Waffen Schutzstaffel (Waffen-SS) but despite their lack of pedigree, they wanted to contribute to their nation's cause. They were fathers, husbands, businessmen, respected members of their community, and came from one of the least Nazified areas of Germany. And they were about to commit the first act of genocide that would establish the little-known 101 Police Battalion as one of the most heinous perpetrators of Hitler's Final Solution.

As the sun broke over the forested landscape, the sky streaked red as the horizon promised a new day. Major Trapp issued the orders that a few NCOs and platoon leaders already knew were coming. With tears in his eyes, Major Trapp explained that the higher-ups had issued an order to kill the Jewish women, children, and elderly in the village. Any Jewish man capable of working would be segregated and transported to a labor camp. His words dumbfounded his men. It didn't make sense. Major Trapp knew the hell he was asking his men to commit, but *war was hell*, he reminded them. Innocent German civilians were being killed in the Allied bombing campaign. Jewish partisans killed German soldiers behind the front lines and then pretended to be civilians. He tried to justify the order to his men, but he knew his words fell short of the complete truth. In a break from tradition, as a conciliatory effort, he offered to any man who was not willing to obey the kill order to step out of ranks. No punishment would follow, he assured them. There would be no consequences for the preservation of their conscience.

One man stepped forward. His true identity is protected; the world only knows this man as Otto-Juluis Schimke—a pseudonym. Out of five hundred men, he was the first to refuse the order to murder. He broke ranks, stepped out of line, and left the herd. Immediately, his company commander berated Otto, embarrassed that one of his men would be the first to act so cowardly. Papa Trapp stopped his captain from yelling at Otto. An estimated ten to twelve more men followed Otto's lead in obeying their conscience and not their orders. They suffered scorn, burning stares, and the isolation of turning their backs on their comrades who allowed duty, honor, and obedience to make them murderers. But those dozen men exercised control of their lives. They decided that authority is only just when the moral and ethical grounds are maintained. They saw the deception taking place. They had eyes for the forgotten. They must have known that understanding what you won't do is just as heroic as knowing what you're able to do.

The operation that followed was performed with quintessential military efficiency and lethality. The village was isolated by two platoons that were tasked to shoot any squirters—someone fleeing out of the village. One platoon would secure the marketplace where the Jews would be initially held until they were transported to the forest. One company would clear the village by searching every single room of every single house to find every single Jewish person. Another company would move to the forest, where it would establish the kill site. There would be no escape. The sick were shot in the beds in which they lay. The battalion doctor instructed the junior officers and senior NCOs on where the victims should be shot so that their deaths would be immediate. Leaders disseminated that information down to the trigger pullers. But the alcohol that was supplied to the policemen later on in the operation to keep them engaged at the necessary rate of murder

CHAPTER 10

unsteadied their aim and caused horrific suffering for their victims.

As three hundred able-bodied Jewish men said goodbye to their families for the last time, they heard the first gunshots ring out from the woods. There was no doubt they were leaving the murder scene of their entire family. The remaining Jewish women, children, and elderly were loaded onto trucks and brought into the woods. They were paired with an executioner, marched into the woods, and told to lie down. They felt the bayonet press against the nape of their neck, and they waited for the bullet that would end their lives.

The killing lasted for hours. The total murder count was between 1,200 and 1,500 Jewish elderly, women, and children. Policemen weary from the butchery that was taking place wanted to stop the shooting, but they were told they could lie down and be shot like the Jews if they wanted to stop. The grace period was over.

If you join the military, you will take an oath to "defend the Constitution of the United States and to defend it against enemies both foreign and domestic" and "to obey the *lawful* orders of the president of the United States and of the officers dually appointed over you." It's worth thinking about what orders would make you step out of the ranks before they happen. Because if you don't know what line you won't cross before others compel you to do so, it will be harder to resist them. You might miss the only chance to follow Otto's example.

If there was ever a need for stoic warriors, it was then, in that exact moment, when twelve men out of five hundred saw into their future that morning and chose a different path. There is always a choice. Your enemy is not whoever you are told to fight. Your enemy is the one you willingly *choose* to fight. Seneca wrote that "All cruelty springs from weakness." Responsibility for what we do starts and stops in our choices as individuals, and we have to be strong enough to find a path away from cruelty. Perhaps the dissent of twelve men didn't even spare one single life that day. But their example serves to future generations as a warning that we obey unlawful orders at our own peril.

A hero knows what truths are worth fighting for and where

fundamentalism or blind obedience to authority begins to creep in. As a young person, you are still forming your thoughts about good and evil. It's a complicated process. I know you want to believe that your country will never put you in a moral and ethical dilemma like the one Otto had to navigate. I know you want to believe that the enemies our government has identified are always going to be evil, bad people. But we are citizens, not subjects. We are participants of the government, not bound to and compelled to obey it without incurring individual responsibility.

Seneca reminds us, "Life is never incomplete if it is an honorable one. At whatever point you leave life, if you leave it in the right way, it is whole." On your heroic journey there will be times when you have to take a stand for what you believe is the right way. Sometimes the consequences of doing so will cost you everything. Your money, your home, your family, and your life can all be taken away from you. Knowing when to take that stand will require all the wisdom you can muster. You won't be perfect, and there will be times when you aren't sure what to believe and who to trust. Is the media presenting information in an unbiased way? Are your professors only instructing you based upon facts or are they teaching their opinion? Are our politicians corrupt? Is the American system of government flawed beyond repair? As you grow older, your ideas about right and wrong will be updated like a new software update on your iPhone.

Stoicism isn't a rigid, fundamental guide to putting the world into black-and-white terms. Stoicism helps me understand my place in a complex world by empowering me with the gift of freedom. Not license, but freedom from myself. Freedom from my anger toward the past, my fear of the future, and my pain in the present. Stoicism has offered meaning to me in circumstances that have been unpleasant, lonely, and stressful. Stoicism has allowed me the gift of questioning myself. Of questioning my responses to circumstances. Should I really be this angry at my roommate because he didn't do his dishes? Should I fly off the handle at work when someone didn't make an important

CHAPTER 10

timeline? Should I trust the feeling I get when I see people with different ideas express their opinions publicly?

Epictetus taught that "No man is free who is not master of himself." By learning to distrust my initial response—my knee-jerk frustrations, greed, envy, anger, and desire—I've learned that I can trust myself more. By recognizing that what I feel is not what I am entitled to act out, I've been able to buy time. I've given my mind the space it needs to maneuver to a better decision. Stoicism made me a smaller person, less important in the world I live in. And that has helped me to become the type of person who is bigger than the old problems I faced. It's given me new tools and new ideas to fall back on when things get difficult.

When you look into the ethical mirror we all have in our consciences, make sure you can meet your own gaze. We are all capable of fooling ourselves in the mirror—my six-pack looks way better in my bathroom mirror with overhead lighting than it does in a photograph of me at the beach with my friends. It's easier to fool myself when I control the narrative. But our conscience shows us the self-evident truths that we violate, and we must learn to listen to its guiding voice when it is telling us we have erred. Marcus Aurelius reminds us: "In all that happens, keep before your eyes those who experienced it before you and felt shock and outrage and resentment at it. Because you can use it, treat it as raw material. Just pay attention and resolve to live up to your own expectations in everything. And when faced with a choice, remember: our business is with things that really matter."

We are going to make mistakes. We are going to fall short of the standards we set for ourselves. We are going to drink too much and piece together the memory of a wild night where we made a fool of ourselves. We'll get angry with friends and family and say things we don't mean. But when we fall short of what we know is the standard of our behavior, we have a choice. Life will present you with opportunities to do the right thing and the wrong thing. What good can you identify that is waiting to be done, and can you become courageous enough to go and do that good?

Epictetus knew that courage was built with the repetition of good choices. He taught, "Practice yourself, for heaven's sake, in the little things and then proceed to greater." Those small acts of courage add up; the goodness we give the world is tipping the scales toward progress, one helping hand at a time.

After reading this book, you no longer have the excuse to let life pass you by. You aren't a bystander anymore. The world needs you to take on the adventure of your life, to become the best version of yourself and to offer the best parts of you to others. Only you and the common thread that has linked your life experiences along the way know what it is you need to do. No one can tell you the hero you ought to be, the causes you need to care about the most, and the profession you have to choose in order to have an impact. Listen to the still-small voice in your head telling you that you can chase that dream.

The measure of the success of your life isn't measured in the tangible accomplishments and success markers that the world has established. It's not about the money or the fame, the status and the popularity, the guts and the glory. Measure yourself against who you once were, and that will guide you into who you could be. And once you've accomplished the goal of who you might become, transform into someone capable of showing others the way. Offer up the lessons of your life so that other people might avoid the mistakes you made.

You will face obstacles. You will face challenges that have stopped people who have come before you in past generations. When you fail, try again. When you err, right your wrongs and move forward. Recommit to change, dust yourself off, and get back on the path. Don't stay fixated on the past, and don't get lost in the fantasy of the future. Rather, use the past and the future as proper guidance on how to navigate the present.

Life is beautiful despite its suffering. No matter how lofty our goals, we still remain a part of the circle of life. We are born, we live, and we die. Heroes live their lives in such a manner that we note their behavior as something worth replicating. We know how our life will end. We know that each and every person we love will die, that we ourselves will not escape the end. So live with the reminder of death's approach as the impetus to cherish the moment. Don't take for granted the people in your life, don't cast aside so easily the relationships that sustain you, and don't give up on the trajectory of your journey when the odds seem all but impossible. The joy—the unbridled, deeply anchored peace of life—that comes when our actions aren't bound by time, when our needs are met, and when we live in abundance acts as the bulwark against the trials coming our way. In short, life makes sense when we are on the heroic journey of our lives.

When this book ends, so too will our time together. But if I've done my job well, there remains only one thing left to be done: for you to take up the mantle. It's your turn. It's your time to step out into the unknown. To make something beautiful of your life. The world is waiting for you to show up and take your place within it.

You'll have to learn the balance between your love life, family, hobbies, education, and career. Put in the work to go to the schools you want. Earn the pride of accomplishing your dreams. Prepare for war. But keep one eye on life. Don't let relationships pass you by. Don't wake up one day and realize that your parents are older and wonder where the time went. Don't look in the mirror one day and not recognize who you are.

Your heroic spirit is a part of you, and it is complimented, not stifled, by exploring the beauty of life. If you enjoy creating and crafting things with your hands, continue creating. If you like teaching, become a better instructor. If you are young and in love and want to start a family, become the best parent and spouse you can be. If you enjoy anything in addition to your calling as a hero do not shun it or spurn it away as weakness. Marcus Aurelius wrote, "Dwell on the beauty of life. Watch the stars and see yourself running with them." Look for the things in life that are beautiful and make them a part of you.

You will grow and change over the years. Chapters of your life will close, sometimes without you knowing they have. How many times have you done something for the last time and not known you were doing it? I remember saying goodbye for the last time to my grandparents before they passed. I remember saying goodbye to my family pets before they were put down. I remember the last times I've shut doors to homes I moved away from. Sometimes the last times we do things are sad times.

When you close this book for good, it will be the last time you have the excuse to not prepare for your heroic calling. This will be the last time you can say if you should become who it is you know you ought to be.

This is the start of your heroic calling. It's the first step you have taken on your heroic journey. As the next generation, the burden of safeguarding freedom, liberty, and justice is in your hands. Keep your head where your heart is and use stoicism as a grounding tool. Create art, code programs, and build businesses in your community. Become a pillar of strength other people rely on and become someone who has an abundance of wisdom to share with those who will listen.

The responsibility is yours. The heroic journey is a young person's game. Eventually, the heavy torch is always passed to the next generation. This is your handoff. Carry it with justice, with temperance, with courage, and with wisdom. I know you can. I believe in you.

Do you?

CONCLUSION

LIFE HAS NO MEANING. EACH OF US HAS MEANING AND WE BRING IT TO LIFE. IT IS A WASTE TO BE ASKING THE QUESTION WHEN YOU ARE THE ANSWER.

—JOSEPH CAMPBELL

A book ends on the last page, but does a story ever really end? Our lives end the moment we take our last breath, but our legacy will live on long after we are gone, with those who once knew us. Our stories are remembered. Our character isn't forgotten.

I struggled to find an ending to this book. It's been a six-year journey. The first version of this book was written in an African desert and revised in snowstorms scattered across the northeastern United States. I started the second version as I hiked the El Camino in Spain and earned the title of a "pilgrim" when I ended my hike at a cathedral. I continued writing versions in cafés in Germany, sipping coffee and staring across beautiful city squares, wondering how many artists, known and unknown, had taken their craft to the same streets. This final draft is written on the continent where it all began. Except this time in Africa, things have been more dangerous than when the book started.

Thanks to the example and admonishment from my favorite author, Steven Pressfield, whenever I have been in the world, I've found my ability to write is linked directly to my ability to put my ass firmly planted where my heart wants to be: behind my keyboard.

As I wrote, COVID-19 emerged and locked down the world. Our country seems to have become irreconcilably divided. I lost an embarrassingly large amount of money in cryptocurrency. I got married to an incredible woman. A business I started when I was twenty-two years old reached one million dollars in equity. I was the second person ever recorded powerlifting 1,000 pounds and running a marathon in the same day. I started therapy, where I go to a farm and speak with a psychologist while the beauty of the countryside acts as a powerful force for healing.

A lot of life has happened since I first embarked on this project. I'm not the same man who started writing so many years ago in Africa, and I am not the same man who will come home from Africa for a second time. My military career has had its ups and downs. I earned my Green Beret and became a member of the Special Forces. Each time I've edited and reread this book, I've had to live up to my words as best as I can.

Now, as I write this conclusion, the Ukraine-Russian war is raging. People are suffering. Innocent people who neither wanted war nor did anything at all to provoke it are suffering the brutal effects of violence. Such is the case not only in Ukraine but in Somalia, Syria, Ethiopia, Sudan, Mexico, and Yemen. Savage aggression is encoded in our DNA as a species. Suffering has been our commandment since the day God threw Adam and Eve out of the Garden. But no matter how cruel the world around us becomes, the helpers can still be found.

Plenty of teenagers had a worse life than I had. Plenty of people will see and do things far more traumatic than I have experienced, not only in the US but around the world; not only in my lifetime, but in the future generations to come. Their wounds will run deeper and hurt more. This book is not about how bad I had it. It is a simple offering to acknowledge that youth can be painful. One day you will realize that life is indeed unfair. I hope that this book finds you before your worldview is challenged. Life will take its daggers to your heart and I hope that you

CONCLUSION

have read this book before that pain comes. If you never transcend that pain, you will be condemned to a lifetime of unnecessary suffering.

Gratitude is the only antidote I've found to such despair. I can't love on demand, I can't forgive immediately, and I don't act perfectly in all situations. But when I am grateful for life—for the breaths I take, for the food I eat, the roof over my head, the freedom I have to live in a free land—I find that there is not much room for anything else. Gratitude sort of pushes out emotions that act as dead weight. But gratitude is a choice. It doesn't come naturally to me any more than someone learns quantum physics. The potential for it is within us, but we must seek it out.

If I've done my job true—if I've I written what is real and stayed as close as possible to life-giving meaning—then maybe one day, when fate presents you with a trial, you will remember a few of the words I've written. You will take some small bit of encouragement with you into the fray. You will find some gratitude in the moment.

If I have led any of you toward the transformation from grief to healing, I will count the years I've put into this book as worth it. No matter what, it was time well spent in service of others.

I hope some part of you learned to dream within these pages, and that the dreams that were born inside you will one day be realized. I hope some part of you grew and matured past the worldviews that would have left you naive and vulnerable to suffering. I hope you know that the world without you would be a worse place. A world that never receives the gift of your meaning manifested will remain unchanged by the good you are meant to offer to it.

Writing a book is a daunting task. It requires perfection. No one tells a writer when they first start writing that the worst part will be editing. That you'll see all of your mistakes, typos, and grammatical errors that were so obviously simple you might wonder if a child wrote it or your adult self. That when you come across your errors you must fix them before small blemishes stain the fabric of the whole work you've woven together for the reader.

But editing the many versions of this manuscript gave me an unexpected gift. It allowed me to reread the work I have done over the years. Each sentence was a snapshot into the mind of the man who once lived years ago, who found some quiet lonely place to sit behind a keyboard and write. Rereading my words, I had to eat them. What wasn't true was cut. What wasn't real was deleted. What was long was made short. What was unclear was refined and distilled down to simple and easily digestible ideas. I killed my darlings like Faulkner commanded.

I thought I was writing for the old me. I started out wanting to write a book that would have helped the sixteen-year-old version of myself navigate the world. To present a resource for that EMT teenager. Instead, as I've read and reread my words, I startled myself by realizing I had crafted a tool I would use in the future.

I hope that the pages of this book become worn and marked and bent and crumpled by use. I hope that you extract all the meaning that there is and hold dear all that you find significant within this story. I hope that years after your first reading of this book, you find it again on a shelf or in a box and blow the dust of the cover and reread it, feeling like you're catching up with an old friend.

If there is only one thing you take away from this book, I hope that it is this: You are the hero of your life. You are the author of your story.

Live out your journey with the bravery of the legends of old and write a story that will outlive the breath inside of you. Sacrifice parts of your life for the service of others, and when your battered and bloody soul heals, offer the strength you have found to those coming behind you. Lend your helping hand to those who are forgotten, and stand over those too defenseless to help themselves, until they are strong enough to replace you in turn.

Take courage. The first steps into the wild unknown of life can be scary; they can be lonely and filled with uncertainty. But you must take those steps.

Edmund Burke wrote that there is a contract among us, between "the dead, the living, and the unborn." You are you—and you are so

CONCLUSION

beautifully unique that there will never be another one of you that will exist in this world. Together we can unite toward a common goal of subtracting from the suffering life imposes.

We are hope. We are the love that can build a better present for our generation, and we are the love that will serve as an example for future generations to do the same.

I am grateful for you. I am grateful for the life you will lead and the things you will do. If we ever meet, tell me about your victories. Show me how far you've come and tell me what the view looks like from the mountain you have climbed. Tell me about the highs and the lows. Show me your scars. And I will celebrate with you.

ACKNOWLEDGMENTS

I'd like to thank Brunella Costagliola, Brannan Sirratt, and Becky Hilliker, the editors who have helped shape and form this manuscript over the years.

And to my wife: thank you for your love and grace. Our life has many more adventures ahead of us.

www.ingramcontent.com/pod-product-compliance
Lightning Source LLC
LaVergne TN
LVHW041950070526
838199LV00051BA/2971